Bridging Our Political Divide

Bridging Our Political Divide: How Liberals and Conservatives Can Understand Each Other and Find Common Ground is an essential contribution to a better national conversation.

Psychologist Kenneth Barish explains the sources and consistency of our political beliefs and why we continue to disagree about fundamental issues in American life. He offers antidotes to the angry, repetitive, and unproductive arguments that now dominate our political culture. Barish teaches us how to listen, think, and speak about our political opinions in a way that allows us to understand each other's concerns, resist false dichotomies and ideological certainty, see new perspectives and possibilities, and find common ground. The concluding chapter shows how we can move beyond partisan divisions toward pragmatic solutions and a better future for America's children.

This fundamentally hopeful book should be read by students in all areas of study, by professionals in the fields of conflict resolution, communication, political science, and social psychology, and by anyone seeking to improve the quality of their conversations with people who may disagree with them, in both politics and in their personal relationships.

Kenneth Barish, Ph.D., is Clinical Professor of Psychology at Weill Cornell Medical College. He is on the faculty of the Westchester Center for the Study of Psychoanalysis and Psychotherapy and of the William Alanson White Institute Child and Adolescent Psychotherapy Training Program, as well as visiting professor at Tongji Medical College in Wuhan, China. He is a fellow of the American Psychological Association and a member of Sigma Xi, the scientific research honor society. In addition to his teaching and clinical practice, Dr. Barish plays jazz trumpet.

"In his beautifully written, lucid, and engaging book, Kenneth Barish addresses the central political, social, and cultural problem of our time: how to bring a fractured and polarized America together so that we, as a nation, can move into a more hopeful future. Barish's book teaches us how to listen with sensitivity and empathy. He offers us a way to understand those with views and values different from our own, making it possible to find common ground. Sensitive and generous, Bridging Our Political Divide gives the reader a sense of hope during these difficult and frightening times."

Thomas A. Kohut, *Sue and Edgar Wachenheim III Professor of History, Emeritus, Williams College, and author of* Empathy and the Historical Understanding of the Human Past

"Kenneth Barish has written the most nuanced and thoughtful discussion about political polarization and the powerful underlying emotions and issues of identity that have transformed what was designed to be a process of vigorous democratic debate into hurtful and often hateful mutual disparagement. He proposes a clear guide to regain the process of dialogue that is so central to a functioning, healthy, and enlivening political process. This book should be read by students, professionals, and the public, to counteract the rapid descent into despair and disillusionment that is tearing families, communities, and our country apart."

Peter Fraenkel, *Ph.D., Associate Professor of Psychology, The City College of New York*

"Ken Barish has accomplished the rare feat of writing a simultaneously erudite and easily digestible book for these polarized times. He offers individuals several ways to restore a sense of mutuality to their personal lives as well as to our communal endeavors. Anyone who can no longer socialize with family or friends whose views differ from their own will appreciate his breakdown of the root causes of our fundamental disagreements and how to find common cause with others when our divergent views deeply alienate us from one another."

Billie A. Pivnick, *Ph.D., co-chair, Center for Public Mental Health, William Alanson White Institute, New York City, NY*

"In his aptly titled, Bridging Our Political Divide: How Liberals and Conservatives Can Understand Each Other and Find Common Ground, Kenneth Barish explores the damage of toxic polarization in modern-day American life. Offering dialogue in place of monologue (debate), he provides a psychologically sound answer to counter the growing chasm in relationships and politics, avoid the destructive abyss of increasing tribalism, and find ways to replace antagonism with teamwork."

Jerrold Lee Shapiro, *Ph.D., Professor of Counseling Psychology, Santa Clara University and author of* Finding Meaning, Facing Fears: Living Fully Twixt Midlife and Retirement

Bridging Our Political Divide

How Liberals and Conservatives Can Understand Each Other and Find Common Ground

KENNETH BARISH

Routledge
Taylor & Francis Group

NEW YORK AND LONDON

Designed cover image: JakeOlimb via Getty Images

First published 2025
by Routledge
605 Third Avenue, New York, NY 10158

and by Routledge
4 Park Square, Milton Park, Abingdon, Oxon, OX14 4RN

Routledge is an imprint of the Taylor & Francis Group, an informa business

© 2025 Kenneth Barish

ISBN: 9781032679068 (hbk)
ISBN: 9781032665894 (pbk)
ISBN: 9781032679075 (ebk)

DOI: 10.4324/9781032679075

Typeset in Dante and Avenir
by KnowledgeWorks Global Ltd.

To my grandchildren – Elliott and Andy – and their generation

Our hope for a better future

Contents

Acknowledgments

I am indebted to many people who have supported me throughout my work on this book.

I cannot possibly thank all the friends, family members, and colleagues who have engaged with me in discussions, challenging me to think more carefully and deeply about the problems I have written about.

I owe a very special thank you to my family editorial team – my wife Harriet and my children Rachel and Dan – who read every word and offered me their loving and honest criticism. This book has benefited immeasurably from their careful reading and insightful critiques.

I am also grateful to other family members and friends who took the time to read the manuscript at different stages and offered valuable recommendations for improvement. Thank you to Steve Barish, Bob Congdon, Mary Beth Congdon, Michael Friedman, Sandy Kessler, Arthur Leaderman, Michael Mascolo, and Steven Smith for helping to make this a much better book.

I would also like to thank my agent, Karen Gantz, for her expert guidance since we first discussed these ideas over dinner at my 50th college reunion.

Finally, thank you to Emilie Coin, my editor at Routledge Press, and her team for believing in the value of this project and working diligently to see it through to completion.

Preface

In a book about the nature of our political differences, I should be open about my own experience and values. I am not involved in the world of politics, except as an informed citizen and student of political psychology who has closely followed political events for many years.

My special expertise is in child psychology and family relationships. In this book, I will draw on my knowledge and experience in these fields. I have spent a good part of every working day, over several decades, helping spouses, parents, and children listen to each other with greater openness and empathy, engage in dialogue, and solve difficult family problems. As a child and family therapist, this has been my life's work.

All the recommendations I will offer for better political conversations are grounded in my daily clinical practice. Our goal, in both therapy with families and for improving our political culture, is to arrest malignant cycles of mutual hostility and contempt and set in motion, in their place, a virtuous cycle of listening, understanding, and problem-solving.

Although I am seeking common ground, I am not entirely impartial. My biases will be apparent, implicit in the examples I choose and the questions I raise, and explicit when I express my personal beliefs.

I will argue that, in politics, as in family relationships, we arrive at our opinions too quickly and hold onto them with unwarranted certainty. I have strong opinions, however, on many issues. My opinions are generally (although not always) liberal. Over time, and in the course of writing this book, I have moderated some of my views. I believe that many liberals have become self-righteous, self-centered, and narrow-minded, and do not make enough effort to understand the concerns and priorities of conservatives. On most issues, however, I am still a liberal.

I have believed in the principles of intellectual charity and intellectual humility, and the importance of understanding problems from multiple perspectives, for most of my adult life. I appreciate their importance even more now, as I get older. I also know, however, that this way of listening and thinking requires a degree of discipline that is difficult to sustain, and, when talking about politics, I cannot always practice what I preach.

Throughout the book, I have made a good-faith effort to honor the principle of intellectual charity and present ideas I disagree with in their most reasonable and persuasive form. Some readers may feel that I have not always been successful and that I have characterized their views unfairly.

I welcome this criticism as an opportunity for understanding our differences more clearly, for learning from each other, and for finding more common ground.

The two parties which divide the state, the party of Conservatism and that of Innovation, are very old and have disputed the possession of the world ever since it was made... The war rages not only in battle-fields, in national councils, and ecclesiastical synods but agitates every man's bosom with opposing advantages every hour...and still the fight renews itself as if for the first time, under new names and hot personalities.

Such an irreconcilable antagonism, of course, must have a correspondent depth of seat in the human constitution. It is the primal antagonism, the appearance in trifles of the two poles of nature.

Ralph Waldo Emerson, *The Conservative*

Introduction

Respectful and constructive dialogue is vanishing from American political life. There is, arguably, no more urgent question for American society today than how we can listen and talk with each other constructively, with less hostility and contempt.

I offer this book as a contribution to better national conversation. It is not a book about who is right and who is wrong. My goal is to help us understand each other, to encourage listening and dialogue, to challenge unproductive modes of thought and debate, and to help us find common ground.

"Downright evil"

The climate of American politics has devolved a long way since Al Gore, in 1992, was able to say about his Republican opponents, "they're not bad people" and George W. Bush appealed for national unity and religious tolerance following the attacks of September 11th.

Many of us no longer feel this way. We are now divided, not only in our political beliefs but in how we feel about each other. We no longer think of the opposing party as people we disagree with; we think, as Gore and Bush told us not to, that they are bad people.

By 2019, over 42% of both Republicans and Democrats believed that members of the other party "are not just bad for politics - they are downright evil."[1]

In some surveys, when asked about actual policies, we disagree with each other about as much as we always have.[2] Our political parties, however, have moved farther apart. Each side sees only the other as becoming more extreme.

Partisanship has a strong effect not only on our opinions but on our perceptions of facts. When the party we support is in office, we believe the economy is doing well. As soon as the other party wins, we believe it is doing badly. (This bias is true of both sides, but more strongly for Republicans.)[3] If we are told that a policy (for example, on welfare benefits) has been proposed by our side, we are likely to agree with it. If we are told that the same policy was presented by the other side, we disagree with it. This process is usually unconscious. We believe that our judgments are based only on the facts and deny that party affiliation has influenced our opinion.[4]

We make gross misjudgments about the other side. Republicans estimate that 32% of Democrats are LGBT (the actual percentage is 6%). Democrats estimate that 38% of Republicans earn over $250,000 a year (the actual percentage is 2%).[5]

We have become a society of "I" not "We." Robert Putnam and Shaylin Romney Garrett have recently documented the transformation of American society, over the past 125 years, from the early 1900s Gilded Age of division and inequality – a society of "I" – to the mid-20th-century society of greater economic equality (with the important exceptions of African Americans and women) and an increasing feeling of "We" – and now, over the past 50 years, back again to a society of "I" – a society with increasingly unequal wealth and a culture of individualism in all spheres of life. This resurgence of individualism over community has been remarkably consistent in all forms of civic life, even the words we use and the names we choose for our children.[6]

An erosion of empathy may be the most important cause (and symptom) of our current polarization and hatred. Arlie Russell Hochschild calls this our "empathy wall." Hochschild asks, "is it possible, without changing our beliefs, to know others from the inside, to see reality through their eyes, to understand the links between life, feeling, and politics; that is, to cross the empathy wall?"[7] Throughout this book, I will offer advice on how we can cross the empathy wall.

I begin with a brief explanation of our political disagreements. Then, I will discuss fundamental principles of constructive dialogue and reasoned argument – attitudes and practices that make political conversations more successful in both our personal and civic lives. I will not discuss political strategy or political messaging – how to persuade voters and win elections. Instead, I will describe a way of listening, thinking, and talking about our political differences that allows us to understand each other's concerns and then, when we continue to disagree, even when we firmly believe that our opponents are wrong, to talk about our disagreements with greater civility and respect.

Three questions

The starting point for the ideas I will present is an observation that has intrigued me for over 50 years. As a college student in the early 1970s, I was puzzled by the consistency of political attitudes across different issues, in different spheres of life. At that time, political leaders who espoused conservative positions on economic and social issues also tended to be hawkish on questions of foreign policy. Liberal politicians, conversely, favored increased spending on social welfare programs and opposed increased military spending and the war in Vietnam. I wondered, then and now, why do these attitudes and opinions go together? What is the logical (or, more likely, emotional) relationship of these different opinions?

This consistency of political opinions, with some exceptions, remains true today, perhaps to an even greater extent, and includes many more issues. Liberals and conservatives differ in their opinions on health care, abortion, immigration, gun control, gay rights, and the threat of climate change. On all of these issues, liberals are (most often) liberal; conservatives are (most often) conservative.[8]

This is the first question. What is the inner coherence of liberal and conservative ideas? What is their "deep grammar"? What is the theme that can be heard throughout many different variations?[9] What are our disagreements really all about?

Are they about different "sensibilities"[10] or "visions" of human nature,[11] different philosophical temperaments[12] or "polarities" of thought?[13] Are our political differences derived from competing moral values[14] or moral "foundations,"[15] from biological predispositions[16] or different "worldviews"?[17] Are they irreconcilable moral visions – an "orthodox" vs. "progressive" morality – engaged in a culture war that cannot be compromised, only decisively won?[18] Or, more cynically, are they more or less elaborate rationalizations for maintaining political power?[19] Or, as I will argue, are they all of these, each true in some respects, but, in other ways, misleading and incomplete?

My first question quickly led to a second question. What is the origin of our conservative or liberal attitudes and opinions? Why do we become liberal or conservative? Why are some of us hawks and some of us doves? Why do some of us passionately believe that a mosque should not be built near the 9/11 Ground Zero site while others, equally passionately, believe that Ground Zero is an ideal location to build a mosque?

These were interesting, but somewhat academic, questions. Over time, what began as a theoretical problem led to a third set of questions and more practical concerns: How can we understand each other and talk together in a more constructive way? Why do friends and family members discuss politics for decades, present arguments and evidence for their views, but remain adamant in their opinions and not change their minds? (Except sometimes they do, and why?)

Why is it hard for us to listen to each other and allow ourselves to be influenced by each other's point of view? Why do we so quickly become defensive and descend to the level of grade school argument?

Why is it difficult for liberals to understand a conservative's fear of crime? Or the need for military preparedness and a strong national defense? Or for liberals to understand conservatives' belief that the

values that have guided their lives (for example, self-reliance, patriotism, and personal responsibility) have been eroded? Or that high
taxes and excessive government regulation may inhibit economic
growth and leave us a poorer, less innovative, country? Or that liberalism can become corrupted, illiberal, and intolerant of free speech?

Why is it difficult for conservatives to understand the devastating effects of poverty on the life chances of children growing
up in conditions of extreme hardship? Or the pain of the families
of Trayvon Martin, Philando Castile, and George Floyd (and many
others)? Or that increasing inequalities of wealth may be destructive of the shared social capital and civic engagement necessary for
a healthy society – a shared sense of purpose – and undermine the
equality of opportunity that has been a core principle of the American
narrative? Or that, in a wealthy society, it feels wrong to many of us
that any person should lose their life savings because they become ill
or that life-saving treatments are available to some and not others?

Why is it difficult for liberals and conservatives to understand
these concerns, even if they propose different answers to these
problems? Why, in our politics, is there so much partisanship,
extremism, hypocrisy, and bad faith?

Reason and emotion

There are many ways to find answers to these questions. We could
begin by asking voters, politicians, and political theorists themselves. We could simply ask liberals and conservatives about the
origin of their beliefs – why they believe what they do. We can study
the writings of liberal and conservative authors and politicians and
look for organizing premises and principles.

When asked why we are liberal or conservative, we will give our
reasons. We are likely to justify our opinions based on evidence and
reflection, on what we have learned from personal experience. To
some extent, the reasons we give for our political opinions must be
real and sincere. Often, however, this cannot be the whole story.

Although we may want to believe otherwise, we are not liberal or
conservative in our head, but in our gut. A Supreme Court justice is

not conservative because he is an "originalist" or a "strict construc-
tionist." He is an originalist because he is conservative. Antonin
Scalia disputed this, even called it a slander, but his argument is
unconvincing. Liberal justices are not liberal because they believe in
a "living constitution." They believe in a living constitution because
they are liberal. For Ruth Bader Ginsburg, the starting point and core
premise of her judicial philosophy was the awareness of injustice.
For Scalia, the starting point was what he perceived as moral deca-
dence in society and the need to defend traditional values. This is
why Scalia and Ginsburg, friends for decades, continued to disagree.

Belief perseverance

Most of us rarely change (or open) our minds when we are presented
with new facts or new arguments. Our resistance to considering
new ideas takes many forms. Once we have formed an opinion or
party allegiance, we seek out only information that confirms our
beliefs. When we are presented with facts contrary to our point of
view, if we cannot prove them false, we find reasons to minimize
their relevance or importance.

This thought process of confirmation bias is evident not only in
politics but in many areas of life. I have observed this bias frequently
in scientific and professional disagreements. If a study (for example,
on the effectiveness of a particular form of therapy) supports our
preconceptions, we uncritically accept the results; if it doesn't, we
scrutinize the methodology.

Nobel Prize-winning psychologist Daniel Kahneman, in a lecture reflecting on his life as a scientist, referred to a similar process he called, "belief perseverance." Kahneman offers this blunt
conclusion:

> As a first approximation, people simply don't change their
> minds about anything that matters. ...the power of reasons
> is an illusion. The belief will not change when the reasons are
> defeated. The causality is reversed. People believe the reasons
> because they believe in the conclusion.[20]

Kahneman argues that belief perseverance is a general principle of human thought. Throughout this book, I will explain why Kahneman is (usually) right and why (sometimes, under optimal conditions) he is wrong.

At times, confirmation bias leads to paradoxical reactions. Information contrary to our beliefs evokes a defensive response that may harden our existing opinions. Becoming more informed about an issue also does not often change our minds. We continue, even more adamantly than before, to disagree. These forms of biased reasoning are not mitigated by education. Susceptibility to believing fake news is just as strong among educated voters as it is among those with less education.[21]

Of course, there are exceptions. We are willing, in some circumstances, to consider events from a different perspective, to modify our attitudes and opinions, and to change our minds. We change (or open) our minds, however, when we change (or open) our feelings.

We are more likely to be open-minded when new facts are presented in the context of open dialogue; when we feel that our needs and feelings have been acknowledged;[22] if we feel respected; and when we are less afraid. In these circumstances, we may still react with defensiveness, but not always, and less so. For coming closer together, we need to cultivate this openness, to the extent possible.

Plan of the book

In Part I, I will answer my first question. I will review theories and research about the nature of our political differences and offer my own synthesis, emphasizing the emotions that are the source of our political beliefs.

In Part II, I will describe essential requirements for successful dialogue – how to strengthen the qualities of relationships that promote greater willingness to listen and softening of our feelings toward people with whom we disagree. These principles are derived from the efforts of many people, in different fields, who have worked to promote understanding and collaboration between opposing groups and from my experience, over several decades, as a child and family therapist.

Better listening is essential, but it is not enough. We also need to learn how to debate. Part III describes rules for more constructive disagreement – how to think and speak about our ideas in a way that allows us to resist false dichotomies and ideological certainty, to see new perspectives and possibilities, and to find common ground.

The principles I will discuss are not intended to create a feeling of kumbaya – moments of togetherness and good feeling that quickly dissipate when conflicts emerge. The kind of conversation I will recommend allows for debate (but it does not begin with debate); it allows for disagreement, for challenging our opponents, for presenting new facts and a different perspective; for pointing out inconsistencies and false assumptions; for disputing the logic and evidence of someone's opinion and whether all the facts have been considered. Argument and debate are valid and necessary forms of political discussion. But, in politics, as in families, it matters how we argue.

In Part IV, I will apply these principles to current political and social issues. I will offer an analysis of ideas presented by prominent liberal and conservative authors and politicians, searching for common ground. In the final chapter, I will discuss proposals presented by writers from different political perspectives about how to solve urgent problems of American society. I will attempt to show how we can move beyond partisan divisions toward pragmatic solutions and a better future for America's children.

Why we disagree   Part I

Meditating on the first and most simple operations of the human soul, I believe that I perceive in it two principles that are prior to reason, of which one makes us ardently interested in our well-being and self-preservation, and the other inspires in us a natural repugnance to seeing any sentient being, especially our fellow man perish or suffer.

Jean-Jacques Rousseau, *Preface to Discourse on the Origin of Inequality*

If you are not a liberal when you're young, you have no heart. If you're not a conservative when you're old, you have no brain.

Often attributed to Winston Churchill

DOI: 10.4324/9781032679075-1

Liberal and conservative **1**

A brief history

In this chapter, I will offer a brief review of several influential theories of liberal and conservative political beliefs. As Emerson observed, conservative and liberal political philosophies have been a consistent feature of human societies for millennia. In Roman politics, the Optimates ("best men") believed in preserving tradition and the existing social hierarchy. They were opposed by the Populares ("favoring the people"), who proposed welfare programs to benefit the poor, limitations on slavery, and an expansion of citizenship rights.[1]

Bertrand Russell, in his *History of Western Philosophy*, finds a similar conflict at the beginning of Western thought. "This conflict existed in Greece before the rise of what we recognize as philosophy ... In changing forms, it has persisted down to the present day, and no doubt will persist for many ages to come."[2]

Conservatism: Tradition and the social order

Historian Patrick Allitt has presented a nonpartisan history of conservatism in British and American politics since the English Glorious Revolution of 1688–1689. Allitt argues that "conservatism is, first of all, an attitude about the world which sees the past as the best guide to navigating our way into the future. Conservatism is a propensity

DOI: 10.4324/9781032679075-2

to keep things the way they are...the preservation of tradition and the current social order."

Conservatives believe that "the really important questions confronting humanity have already been answered...[and that] blueprints for transforming society will not work." Conservatives are "writers and politicians ...[who] sought to preserve the advantages of the political stability in England and America against external threats." Allitt notes that during this long period of British and American history, conservatism has most often been reactive. Conservatives "valued the world as they found it...[and] they reacted to what they perceived as threats confronting it."

Allitt's understanding of conservative political ideas – conservatism as a reaction to perceived threats, "valuing the world as they found it" – has considerable support in contemporary social science research. Allitt notes that this understanding of conservatism helps explain the changing nature of conservative ideas over time and solves some apparent paradoxes and exceptions. In the era of the French Revolution, conservatives were monarchists; in a later era, conservatives supported slavery and opposed the extension of suffrage to non-property owners and women. No respectable contemporary conservative holds these views. But the fundamental nature of conservatism has not changed. Contemporary conservatives are reacting to different perceived threats to the current social order.[3]

Allitt's understanding of conservatism, however, immediately raises a problem. "The way things are" is often cruel and unjust. Liberalism begins here, with "an abhorrence of cruelty"[4] and a questioning of established authority – in religion, philosophy, and politics.[5]

Contemporary political essayist Adam Gopnik argues that the defining feature of political liberalism is humanism. Gopnik writes that the liberal tradition in politics is "a history of humane social reform, one of the great moral adventures in human history... responsible for almost all of the humane changes that the Western world has seen in the past two hundred years."[6]

If this seems too grand a claim for liberalism (and perhaps it is), equally grand claims are often made for conservatism. Conservative philosopher Roger Scruton, for example, wrote that conservatism is a "great tradition" that safeguards the achievements of civilization from destruction by revolution and totalitarianism.[7] Almost all conservative political philosophy and conservative politicians share this conviction, in different forms – that conservatism is necessary to protect what is best in society from the excesses of liberalism. The greater the perceived threat or excess, the more impassioned the conservative reaction; in a similar way, the greater the perceived cruelty or injustice, the more impassioned the liberal desire for change.

Tough-minded and tender-minded personalities

William James proposed a well-known dimension of personality – tough-minded and tender-minded temperaments – to describe a fundamental difference between philosophers of different schools of thought. James wrote,

> The history of philosophy is to a great extent that of a certain clash of human temperaments. [The philosopher]…when philosophizing, urges impersonal reasons…[but] He *trusts* his temperament [and]…the potentest of all our premises is never mentioned.

James continued,

> They have a low opinion of each other….The tough think of the tender as sentimentalists and soft-heads. The tender feel the tough to be unrefined, callous, or brutal…Each type believes the other to be inferior to itself.[8]

Contemporary liberals and conservatives often talk about each other in the same mutually contemptuous way as James' tender-minded and tough-minded philosophers. Could this be the defining difference? Perhaps. On almost every issue that separates liberals and conservatives in contemporary America – immigration; foreign relations; health care; welfare; LGBTQ rights; and gun control – conservatives are tough-minded and liberals are tender-minded. Ronald Reagan and Margaret Thatcher were famously tough-minded politicians. Bill Clinton, equally famously, told voters that he could feel their pain.

Ideological polarities: Feelings vs. norms

Psychologist Sylvan Tomkins proposed a similar theory of political ideologies, based on what he considered a basic polarity in human thought. Tomkins distinguished left-wing ideologies, based on the primacy of feelings (humanism) vs. right-wing ideologies, based on the primacy of behavioral norms, rules, and traditions ("normativism"). He noted that these opposing ideologies can be found throughout history, beginning in ancient Greece, in the philosophies of Protagoras and Plato.[9]

Visions of human nature

Economist and political scientist Thomas Sowell proposed that our political differences are based on different "visions" of human nature and society – different core assumptions about the causes of social stability and social change. A vision is "our sense of how the world works." Different visions "differ fundamentally as to the sources of human survival and progress."

Writers with what Sowell calls an "unconstrained" (generally liberal) vision seek solutions to social problems. In the unconstrained vision, there are no intractable reasons for social evils and therefore no reason why they cannot be solved with sufficient moral commitment. In contrast, writers with a "constrained" (generally conservative) vision believe that solutions are unachievable because of the inherent limitations of human nature. These writers argue that efforts to solve social problems will, at best, have unforeseen costs and will benefit some people but harm others. Sowell explains, "While believers in the unconstrained vision seek the special causes of war, poverty, and crime, believers in the constrained vision seek the special causes of peace, wealth, or a law-abiding society."

The constrained vision is a tragic perspective on human life; the unconstrained vision is a more optimistic view. In more common terminology, those who have a constrained vision are realists; those with an unconstrained vision are idealists. Sowell explains, for example, that in the unconstrained vision, "the amassing of military power by a peaceful nation is dangerously counterproductive." In the constrained vision, it is "absolutely essential to preserve peace," and unprovoked aggression, whether by nations or individuals, cannot be "rooted out by better understanding" but, instead, must be deterred.

Sowell adds an important qualification: "These will be abstractions of convenience, recognizing that there are degrees in both visions, that a continuum has been dichotomized." "Virtually no one believes that man is 100 percent unconstrained and virtually no one believes that man is 100 percent constrained," and "neither vision can confidently claim the air of incontrovertible truth which some of its eighteenth-century exponents exhibited."[10]

If Sowell is right, this should give us some hope. Society needs both realists and idealists. Most of us have some ideal vision of a better world. Most of us temper our idealism with realistic constraints.

Moral politics

George Lakoff, a cognitive scientist, also asks the questions I began with. Lakoff asks, "Can we explain what unifies the collections of liberal and conservative positions? What does opposition to abortion have to do with opposition to environmentalism? What does either have to do with affirmative action or gun control or the minimum wage?"

Lakoff tells us that he was drawn to the study of politics by this intellectual puzzle. He proposes a very different answer than Thomas Sowell. Unlike Sowell, Lakoff believes that liberal and conservative political opinions are derived not from different visions, but from different moral values. He writes, "our political division is a moral division."[11]

Lakoff argues that conservatism is based on a "strict father" morality – a morality that values obedience to authority. Liberalism, in contrast, is derived from a "nurturant parent" morality that values empathy. In Lakoff's view, this fundamental division between strictness and nurturance lies behind our differences on all individual issues.

As in Sowell's visions, there is reason for hope in Lakoff's ideas, because most parents are (and should be) both nurturant *and* strict. We have known for half a century that children are more likely to thrive when parents are able to balance these concerns and raise their children with both warmth *and* authority.[12] And most citizens, except extreme ideologues, recognize the need for both compassion and safety in the maintenance of a just and well-functioning society.

Moral foundations

Jonathan Haidt has conducted important research on the moral foundations of our political and religious differences. Haidt argues (along with many others) that political opinions are based less on reasoned arguments and, instead, on moral "intuitions." He explains, "Intuitions come first, strategic reasoning comes second." Haidt compares the relationship of intuition and reasoning to an elephant and rider; the rider (rational thought) has some influence, but the elephant (our intuitions) usually decides where to go. He offers this understanding of the relationship of emotion and reason in morality and politics: "We do moral reasoning not to reconstruct the actual reason why *we ourselves*...came to a judgment; we reason to find the best possible reasons why somebody else ought to join us in our judgment."[13]

In Haidt's theory, political attitudes are based on five distinct moral foundations (or six, in subsequent research). He describes moralities of (1) Care, (2) Fairness, (3) Loyalty, (4) Authority, and (5) Sanctity. Each of these foundations has its origin in different human social needs and conferred some advantage to the survival of human groups. Haidt finds that liberals primarily endorse the moral foundations of Care and Fairness; Loyalty, Authority, and Sanctity are much less important. Conservatives, however, use all five moral foundations. He labels this "the conservative advantage."[14]

Moral Foundations theory offers a somewhat different grammar for how people feel and think about political issues – and therefore more ways to listen to each other's concerns. All of us, at times, make use of each foundation, to a greater or lesser degree. Haidt suggests that moral foundations theory may especially help liberals better understand conservatives, for example, to appreciate the advantages of authority and leadership for the survival of human groups, especially when our lives are threatened.

Are we born this way?

Social science has also attempted to answer my questions. There is now extensive research on the nature and origins of our political differences. The most surprising fact that has emerged from this research is the role of genetics in political beliefs. We are "predisposed" toward liberal or conservative attitudes in both politics and culture. Correlations in political attitudes of identical twins are significantly higher than for fraternal twins. Identical twins raised apart, in different families, are very similar in their political beliefs; fraternal twins raised apart are not.[15]

These findings are challenging to both sides. When asked why we are liberal or conservative, we may cite our upbringing, our values, or our reasoned assessment of current social conditions. All of these, of course, influence our political opinions. Very few of us, however, are likely to answer, "I was born this way."

Our political nature

Political psychologist Avi Tuschman reviews extensive research on current political attitudes and their possible evolutionary origins. He argues that *political orientations are natural dispositions... molded by evolutionary forces.*[16] Tuschman identifies three universal dimensions of personality that influence political attitudes:

Tribalism, Attitudes toward Inequality, and Perceptions of Human Nature. He argues that each of these dimensions has its origin in human evolution.

Tuschman's first dimension is tribalism. We depend on our social groups for our survival. People with a tribal orientation to life are more ethnocentric, more religious, and more intolerant of sexual differences. Conservatives consistently obtain high scores on measures of tribalism. Tuschman contrasts tribalism (xenophobia) with its opposite, what he calls, "xenophilia" – the desire to engage with members of other groups. He notes that xenophilia also has evolutionary advantages, strengthening our resilience as a species in coping with changes in environmental conditions.

Tuschman's second core personality disposition, related to, but distinct from, tribalism, is "tolerance for inequality." Differing attitudes toward inequality between conservatives and liberals is a consistent finding of social science research. Conservatives show greater acceptance of all forms of inequality – inequality between genders, between racial groups, and between rich and poor. In contrast, liberals believe in the inner equality of all people. For the liberal mindset, this is a central, defining political conviction.

Tuschman's third dimension of political attitudes is "perceptions of human nature." Conservatives espouse a more competitive view of human nature (as in Hobbes' famous dictum that human life is "nasty, brutish, and short"). Liberals are likely to believe in a more cooperative view of human nature. Of all the many unproductive arguments between liberals and conservatives, this debate seems especially silly. How could anyone doubt that human survival has required instincts for both competitive and cooperative relationships?

Research in political psychology has established a catalog of personality differences between liberals and conservatives. Here are some examples: John Hibbing and colleagues report, "Across a range of topics ... liberals consistently favored the new experience, the abstract, and the nonconforming. Conservatives just as consistently favored traditional experiences that were closer to reality and predictable patterns. Conservatives, for example, preferred their poems to rhyme and fiction that ended with a clear resolution."[17]

In experimental situations, conservatives and liberals differ in their unconscious emotional reactions. Conservatives, for example, look longer at threatening images and show greater physiological responses to images that evoke disgust. Other research has identified differences between liberals and conservatives on measures of fear and the need for protection from perceived threats;[18] and the need for certainty.[19]

Hibbing and colleagues propose that our core biological predispositions are openness (liberalism) and fear (conservatism). Liberals, who approach political life from an attitude of openness, are more likely to favor social change, to support greater tolerance for difference and engagement with out-groups, and to believe in a more democratic, egalitarian society (and more egalitarian relationships in general, for example, in families). Conservatives, who approach politics and society from an attitude of fear, are more likely to believe in preserving tradition and the importance of authority, in loyalty to in-groups and wariness toward out-groups, and are less troubled by social inequalities.

A Rosetta Stone for understanding political differences?

Marc Hetherington and Jonathan Weiler have presented a similar framework for understanding political differences, also based on recent social science research. Hetherington and Weiler argue that conservatives and liberals have different "worldviews" that influence their opinions and preferences on a wide range of issues. In this model, alertness to threat is fundamental to a "fixed" (conservative) worldview; in contrast, "the appeal of the new and novel, and welcoming ... people who look and sound different" is central to a "fluid" (liberal) worldview.

Hetherington and Weiler propose that a person's worldview can be identified on the basis of their answer to a single question regarding physical safety or danger. The question they pose is: "Our lives are threatened by terrorists, criminals, and illegal immigrants and our priority should be to protect ourselves" vs. "It's a big, beautiful world, mostly full of good people, and we must find a way to embrace each other and not allow ourselves to become isolated." They report that "nearly 80 percent of Donald Trump supporters chose the first statement. Nearly 80 percent of Hillary Clinton supporters agreed with the second."

A person's worldview is reflected especially in his or her parenting values. When presented questions about the qualities they most want their children to have and asked to choose between alternatives, people with a fixed worldview more often choose obedience, respect for elders, good manners, and good behavior. People with a fluid worldview choose independence, self-reliance, curiosity, and being considerate. With these questions, Hetherington and Weiler believe they have found "something of a Rosetta stone in understanding contemporary American public opinion."

Hetherington and Weiler propose that "At its root, someone's worldview is a reflection of their primal alertness to the relative safety or danger of their environment." The perception of threat – that the world is a dangerous place – reinforces values needed to protect ourselves and survive in a threatening environment – toughness, barriers, hierarchy, conformity, obedience to authority, tradition, and certainty. [20]

These research findings are an important contribution to understanding the origins of our political beliefs. Predispositions, however, are only predispositions. Researchers in political psychology acknowledge the limitations of biological and personality variables as explanations for why we disagree. Hibbing and colleagues note that the correlations observed in research on political psychology, although reliable, are often modest. And, of course, people change their minds. Many prominent conservative politicians in the modern era were once liberals or socialists. Ronald Reagan is probably the most well-known example of this change of mind and heart, but there are many others.

Hibbing and colleagues conclude that "biopolitics" has the equivalent of a pair of nines – in five-card stud poker, a winning hand about half the time. In the next chapter, I will discuss other ways of understanding our political differences. I will offer a synthesis that helps explain liberal and conservative opinions not only in politics but also in other areas of life.

If we draw a few more cards, we may end up with a better hand.

Beyond politics $\qquad$ **2**

The essence of liberalism and conservatism

In this chapter, I will present a general theory of liberalism and conservatism that incorporates the historical observations and modern social science research reviewed in Chapter 1. I will begin with examples of liberal and conservative attitudes in areas of life beyond politics.

I offer the following hypothesis: *At the most general level, liberalism and conservatism are expressions of an inherent tension in human nature between the instincts of empathy (compassion) and self-preservation (security) and reflect the feelings, concerns, values, and social priorities animated by these different human instincts.*

Rousseau and Churchill would agree.

This understanding of liberal and conservative political opinions may seem intuitive and self-evident to some readers. However, it is likely to face strenuous objections and evoke defensiveness in others who believe that their political opinions – or the opinions of their opponents – are based on different motivations and reasons.

Liberalism and conservatism in language, science, and religion

My original questions and most of the examples I have mentioned so far focus on political (and, to a lesser extent, cultural) attitudes and beliefs. Liberalism and conservatism, however, are not limited

DOI: 10.4324/9781032679075-3

to politics. Liberal and conservative impulses and sensibilities are present in science and religion, in music and art, in how we raise our children, and in every organization or institution.

Language

Liberalism and conservatism are present even in languages. Languages that have few native speakers (and are therefore in danger of becoming extinct) become "conservative" and "xenophobic" – they do not readily admit foreign words into their vocabulary. Words or expressions from foreign languages are perceived as an existential threat – a threat to the survival of the language as a distinct entity.

In contrast, languages spoken by many people (for example, English) commonly make use of words from foreign sources. In English, we have little difficulty admitting foreign words into our lexicon, because English is not an endangered language. English speakers will talk about a rendezvous, a tsunami, or the emotion of schadenfreude. These have become English words. Our existential security allows us to be more open; we can afford to be more liberal.

This example can be extended to other aspects of culture and offers an exact parallel to politics. Language, like art and music, has liberal innovators, open to new forms of expression. They are opposed by traditionalists, who believe that something valuable is lost when we too readily change our linguistic usage, that new usages erode or degrade the uniqueness of our (in this case, linguistic) culture.

French offers an interesting example, an apparent exception that proves the rule. An everyday French speaker frequently uses English expressions. She may say, for example, "le week-end" or more recent anglicisms ("software" or "e-mail"). The French Academy, however, founded with the explicit conservative mission (dare I say, raison d'etre) of preserving the integrity of the French language, opposes most anglicisms. This process, debated relatively harmlessly in the realms of language, art, and philosophy, is more dangerously present in our current culture wars and efforts at censorship[1] and cultural "purification."[2]

Science

Liberal and conservative biases are also present in science. The reaction of 19th-century biologists to the theory of evolution is perhaps the most well-known example of scientific liberalism and conservatism. Liberal scientists responded with openness to Darwin's theory; conservative scientists regarded evolution not only as a new scientific hypothesis but as a threat to the social and moral order.[3] This controversy is of more than historical interest. A 2019 study, using a variety of research methods, found that only 54% of the U.S. population believes in the theory of human evolution.[4]

Religion

Liberalism and conservatism in religions show all these defining characteristics. Liberal Christians and Jews are more willing to accept changes in rituals and traditions. Their openness to change defines their liberalism. Conservatives in each of these religions place greater value on preserving tradition; again, change is thought (or felt) to be a threat to the integrity and survival of the religion. This belief defines their conservatism.

Conservativism in religion (especially, religious fundamentalism) almost always seeks to maintain authority, hierarchy, dogma, and differentiated gender roles. The film *The Two Popes*[5] depicts the personal and theological conflict between conservative and liberal priorities in the Catholic Church – the defense of authority and dogma vs. compassion for those left out. The controversy between conservative and liberal Catholics regarding the papacy of Pope Francis is paradigmatic of this clash of liberal and conservative temperaments and beliefs. This is a contemporary example of Emerson's "primal antagonism," a tension also evident between liberal and orthodox Jews and, perhaps, in all religions.[6]

Preserving our identity

This perspective on liberal and conservative opinions suggests, as Emerson believed, that *liberalism and conservatism represent a fundamental tension in our emotional lives, present in all of us.*

Liberals and conservatives differ in how much openness, change, and assimilation feel right to us and to what extent change is felt as an existential threat. We are often faced with conflicts and dilemmas of this kind, in many aspects of our lives, some more consequential than others, as individuals and, especially, as members of institutions and social groups. The specific concerns and issues are different in every case, but the theme is the same, present in many variations: How much can we change and still preserve the distinctiveness of our institutions and our culture? How open can we be to new ideas and practices and still preserve our identity?

Liberalism, in all spheres of life, is characterized by openness. As we have seen, there is now an abundance of social science research on the personality characteristics of self-identified liberals and conservatives. Liberals consistently obtain higher scores on measures of openness to new experiences.

A common meaning of the word liberal is to allow, or allow in. Liberal thought allows new ideas in. Liberal politics allows others in. In social and political life, liberalism is animated by a particular kind of openness – empathy, our openness to the feelings of others, especially the perception of suffering and injustice. When we are liberal, we allow others into our circle of concern. The larger and more inclusive our circle of concern, the more liberal we become.

In contrast, conservatism – in politics, science, and the arts, in religion, and in all institutions – is animated by a perceived threat to something valued. We become conservative when we believe that something essential to our way of life – our status, our values, our culture, our identity – is threatened. We are conservative to the extent that we find meaning and security in traditions and existing institutions *and believe that these traditions or institutions are endangered.*

This does not mean that liberals are always empathic and that conservatives are always callous. For all of us, there are limits to our empathy and conditions in which our empathy is restricted or attenuated. No one is capable of always being empathic, compassionate, or concerned about the well-being of others, of always extending our circle of concern to others whose life circumstances and relationship with us (biological or cultural) are distant from our own.

There is an inherent tension between these two cognitive-emotional systems. We have evolved emotional and cognitive biases for both empathic concern and the perception of danger. The threat we perceive may be imagined or it may be real, or it may be real but exaggerated.

Threat erodes empathy and increases our capacity for cruelty. Empathy softens the harshness of our judgments and our actions. In threatening circumstances, we draw a stronger boundary between ourselves and others. We build a wall, emotionally or physically.

The essence of liberalism

Political liberalism seeks to improve the lives of those who are suffering, not thriving, or excluded under the current social, economic, and political structure. Suffering and injustice are the starting points of political liberalism.

The fundamental premise of political liberalism is this: People are suffering. Current conditions are unjust. This is wrong. We (all) need to help them, now. In his manifesto, *Conscience of a Conservative*, Barry Goldwater criticized liberals for this attitude.[7] Liberals, he wrote disapprovingly, are "in a hurry." And the answer from liberals is, "Yes, we are."

George Lakoff has argued for this understanding of political liberalism. Lakoff offers this thesis: "Behind every progressive policy lies a single moral value: empathy..."[8] Adam Gopnik presents a similar understanding. Liberalism, in Gopnik's analysis, is animated by "an abhorrence of cruelty."[9]

Critiques of liberalism that do not understand this – that identify liberalism, for example, with a belief in "big government" or a philosophy of "expressive individualism" or with a belief in the perfectibility of human nature – misunderstand the essence of liberalism. These beliefs may be features of some forms of liberalism, but they are not the defining feature; all these ideas about liberalism are partially correct but miss the most essential point.

The historical achievements of liberalism – democracy (opposed by conservatives in the 18th century); the abolition of slavery (opposed by conservatives, especially in the United States); the extension of voting rights to non-property owners and women; laws limiting child labor; universal public education; universal health insurance (in the United States, for the elderly; in most other wealthy nations, for the general public); laws against discrimination on the basis of race, sex, or religion – achievements that are no longer controversial but were adamantly opposed by conservatives of other times – are all animated by empathy.

The goals of contemporary liberalism in the United States – universal health insurance; restrictions on gun ownership; the right to have an abortion; efforts to reduce the potentially catastrophic effects of climate change; a path to citizenship for undocumented immigrants; an increase in the minimum wage; opposition to the death penalty; an emphasis on diplomacy in foreign relations – are also animated by empathy.

When our thoughts and feelings are influenced by empathy, we think and feel about others as essentially like ourselves, less as different, as "others." We are more willing to "feel their pain." We make less of a distinction between "us" and "them." We are less tribal, more universalist, and less threatened by people who are in some way different from ourselves.

When we are empathic, we are more likely to be "soft" or "tender-minded," not wanting to cause pain or injury. As parents, we do not want our children to feel disappointed or sad; we want to comfort rather than scold. For this reason, we are more likely to be permissive rather than strict and to give in (perhaps more than we should).

This does not mean that liberal policies are always wise or correct. Liberalism may be misguided, or excessive, or lead to policies and actions that produce results contrary to what is intended. Liberal ideas and values can become corrupted. The openness and compassion of liberals may be naïve, even dangerously naïve. The potential naivete of liberalism is not a trivial complaint. Naivete, especially in international relations, can be catastrophic.

These are all legitimate critiques of the liberal mindset and liberal policies. But political liberalism begins here. This is also a common understanding of liberalism among the general public. Liberals are called "bleeding hearts" (or, more derisively, "tree huggers"). Many liberals proudly accept this label.

The essence of conservatism

The fundamental premise of political conservatism is this: My freedom (our freedom), my way of life, is being threatened. We need to defend it. To the extent that we believe that our way of life – our existence, our freedom, our ideals, or something we deeply value – is endangered, we become conservative.

The perception of threat is the common theme among the many different conservatisms – the threat to traditions and the institutional stability that is derived from them (traditionalists); the threat to free enterprise (economic conservatives); to our social status; to our national security; to law and order; and the threat to moral order (social conservatives). *The greater the perceived threat, the greater the conservative response.*

As a feeling of threat increases, so does tribalism – the awareness of differences among groups and the tendency to see others as members of groups (that is, as "us" vs. "them") as well as efforts at purification, the need for authority, and, in religion, for orthodoxy.[10]

Volkans's tent

Psychoanalyst and diplomat Vamik Volkan offers an analogy:[11] Volkan compares our ethnic identity to a large canvas tent. The fabric of the tent is made from our culture – our language, dress, and cuisine, our customs and rituals. Under conditions of relative security, these traditions constitute a large part of our identity;

they are a source of meaning and enrich our lives. But we are also open to learning from other cultures, incorporating new ideas and practices, and modifying our own.

Under conditions of threat, especially when we feel that our identity is threatened, we instinctively attempt to strengthen the tent, in different ways. We strengthen the outer fabric, investing more in our distinctive culture and expelling foreign influences. We also strengthen the pole that holds up the tent. In Volkan's model, the pole of the tent represents our leaders. We look to strong leaders to protect us. The pole of the tent can also be other sources of authority – our Constitution (we become originalists) or the Bible (we become literalists).

A perceived threat to our way of life often evokes aggressiveness in our self-defense. Aggressiveness, in these instances, is one aspect of our instinctive reaction to threat – the more we feel threatened, the more aggressive we are likely to become. As threat increases, as people feel that their way of life is endangered, so does the potential for cruelty (or looking away from cruelty).

Liberalism and conservatism: Essential truths

From this perspective, we can find important truths in both liberalism and conservatism. Conservatism, in its moderate forms, contains an essential truth: We need to defend ourselves. The guiding principle of conservative political leaders and conservative political philosophy is this: I will protect you from them – from foreign enemies, from domestic crime, from immoral or undeserving others, and from threats to your status in society. I will fight to preserve our way of life – our traditions and distinctions. Protection from threats to our way of life is the unifying theme of conservative domestic and foreign policy. When our way of life is threatened, we all become more conservative.

Liberalism is also based on an essential truth: We need to eliminate cruelty, suffering, and injustice, and to care for others. The guiding principle of liberal political leaders is this: I will work to end poverty, hardship, and injustice.

Many conservatives will object to this characterization of liberalism and conservatism. They may be offended by the implication that they are conservative because they are less empathic or "don't care" about suffering and injustice. These writers offer pragmatic reasons for their conservatism. They believe that conservatism is equally empathic as liberalism but recognizes the need for a strong national defense and a society based on law and order; that their conservatism is based on a defense of freedom (Barry Goldwater and Ronald Reagan famously expressed this idea); that the best way to alleviate poverty is through a vigorous, lightly regulated capitalism; or that, without small government and a balanced budget, we will be unable to afford compassionate assistance to the poor.

George Will, in a recent summation of his life's work, presents a contemporary conservative political philosophy that incorporates many of these ideas.[12] Will argues that we are both more prosperous – and better people – with limited government regulation of our lives. He believes that excessive government regulation strangles individual initiative, promotes a culture of dependency, and erodes a sense of personal responsibility. In Will's view, inequality is inevitable; we should strive, instead, for freedom – freedom of opportunity, not equality of outcomes. Progressivism, in Will's understanding, is based on the naïve (and arrogant) belief in the perfectibility of human nature and an equally naïve (and arrogant) faith in the benevolence and wisdom of government.

These are important ideas that need to be thoughtfully considered. But, for an understanding of the nature of liberalism and conservatism, there is a problem. From the perspective of recent American and British history, compassion has been, at best, a secondary concern of conservative political parties.[13] Thomas Sowell, despite his belief that differences between liberals and conservatives are not based on different value premises, acknowledges that concern for the poor is largely absent from the writings of conservative political theorists.

There is another, even more controversial, problem. Conservatism must face the frequent association of conservative political ideology with xenophobia and racism. This is an especially fraught question, evoking agreement from many liberals and outrage from conservatives.

Avi Tuschman presents evidence that xenophobia (ethnocentrism) is a significant component, perhaps the core, of modern conservatism. Tuschman notes that, "In every country, the right is more ethnocentric than the left." He reports that people who identify themselves as conservative are far more likely to endorse negative racial stereotypes, not only in the United States but also in Europe and Israel. In a study of 4000 Europeans, conservatism was the best predictor of xenophobia and ethnic prejudice.[14] Far-right political parties in Europe and America acknowledge and justify their xenophobia. This, of course, is anathema to liberals.

Tuschman also reports that conservatives have "more positive feelings toward their in-groups and higher levels of patriotism toward their country. In the United States, they are more likely to have a flag in their bedroom."[15] Many American liberals will be offended by the suggestion that they are less patriotic than conservatives. They will reply that they are equally patriotic in their support of American ideals (although perhaps less nationalistic in their approach to foreign relations), that their patriotism takes a different form.

It seems undeniable, however, that the *feeling and centrality* of patriotism and national pride is more common among conservatives. Conservatives in the United States are more deeply offended, for example, by athletes who kneel in protest during the national anthem and by criticisms of American foreign policy (what some conservatives call, "America bashing"). American liberals are far more likely to criticize America – in international affairs and the history of our country. A liberal will almost never say, as many American conservatives did during the war in Vietnam, "Love it or leave it" or "My country, right or wrong, my country."

On these issues, Tuschman's data and analysis justify the following conclusion: If patriotism is the positive side of tribalism, xenophobia and racism are an ever-present danger.

Emotion, reason, and values

From these core emotional biases – compassion and threat – we construct systems of thought – ideas, values, philosophies, and jurisprudence. This is the source of our visions, sensibilities, worldviews, and moral foundations.[16] The primacy of emotion in political beliefs is present in the quotation from Rousseau at the beginning of this section (that the principles of compassion and self-preservation are "prior to reason"). Compassion and self-preservation are where our ideas begin. This is why, in the 18th century, Thomas Paine, beginning with injustice and concern for "have-nots," was a liberal, and Edmund Burke, beginning with a fear of anarchy, was a conservative.[17]

The instincts of compassion and self-preservation give rise to different values. Liberal values are based on empathy and the need to care for others – tolerance and equality. Conservative values are the qualities we need to protect ourselves from perceived threats – loyalty, obedience, respect for authority, strength (and, perhaps, purity). When individuals or groups feel threatened, when the world seems dangerous, these qualities – as individuals, in our leaders, and in our children – become more highly valued. Our worldview is conservative or liberal to the extent that these values have become deeply embedded in our personalities and our opinions.

Liberalism and conservatism: Moderate and extreme

This perspective on liberalism and conservatism helps us understand moderate and extreme forms of political ideology. A common source of our difficulty talking constructively with each other derives from our tendency to see our opponents as extremists, a monolithic group that we despise or fear.

In its moderate forms, conservatism accepts gradual social change and seeks to achieve compassionate ends by conservative means (without changing the fundamental structure of social relations or traditions). In its moderate forms, conservatism is strict but forgiving.

In its extreme forms, conservatism is authoritarian, intolerant, xenophobic, fundamentalist, and harshly punitive. In its extreme forms, conservatism denies the existence of injustice. Or doesn't care. In their extreme forms, conservative political ideas are more or less disguised justifications for the protection of privilege and social hierarchy. Historically, this form of conservatism is almost self-evident. In the era of the French Revolution and in antebellum America, conservatives "believed in" the divine right of kings or biblical justifications for slavery.

In its moderate forms, liberalism appreciates the meaningfulness of traditions and the need for social order – but not at the expense of injustice. In its moderate forms, liberalism is tolerant of differences in values and ways of life and supports institutions necessary to preserve these rights.

In its extreme forms, liberalism denies the legitimacy of current institutions and regards them as evil. The greater the felt illegitimacy of institutions, the greater the extremism. In its radical forms, liberalism believes that institutions are always wrong and aggrieved individuals are always right. (In its radical forms, conservatism believes the opposite.)

In the next chapter, I will discuss, in more detail, the core emotions that animate and sustain our political beliefs – the emotions of resentment, humiliation, pride, and fear.

Political emotions

3

The politics of resentment, humiliation, pride, and fear

One of the major themes of this book is that we are motivated in our political opinions first by feelings and secondarily by ideas or beliefs. Our political opinions begin with what *feels* right or wrong to us. Because our opinions are derived from feelings, to understand why we disagree – and how we can talk with each other more constructively – we need to understand why our opponents feel the way they do.

Political feelings and attitudes have their source in our need for safety and security, for acceptance and belonging, by compassion for the suffering of others, and by our anger at injustice. We are often motivated by an instinctive (but modifiable) fear of others; by our need for a feeling of pride, in some form; and by feelings of resentment and humiliation. We are also motivated, although perhaps less strongly, by our search for positive emotions – by hope and by our need for a feeling of goodness and gratitude that we want to preserve for ourselves and extend to others.

In contemporary America, we are increasingly divided by feelings of resentment, humiliation, and fear. On the right, our current politics is dominated by grievances – that undeserving others are getting what we have worked hard for, that liberal values are destroying the moral foundation of society, and that children are being taught to dishonor and hate the country they should be proud of. These grievances have become increasingly malignant,

DOI: 10.4324/9781032679075-4

spreading for several decades, from the bottom-up, as feelings of disrespect, and from the top-down, by demagogues and partisan media, now justifying efforts at censorship and threats of violence against those who disagree.

On the left, political attitudes are dominated by a different set of grievances – a feeling of injustice that, in many instances, has also become malignant – an arrogant and self-righteous demand, also justifying censorship (and self-censorship, through fear) and acts of "cancellation," jeopardizing the careers of decent people who may have chosen the wrong word or who simply disagree.[1]

Extreme and dangerous political attitudes, however, most often originate with an understandable concern. If we can talk about these feelings at their source, as a response to real events, we have a chance to arrest this malignant process.

The politics of resentment

Political scientist Francis Fukuyama has presented an analysis of the emotional forces influencing political history and our current moment. Fukuyama believes that to understand contemporary political events, we need a better theory of the human soul.

Drawing from Hegel's philosophy of history, Fukuyama argues that politics is animated by more than economic self-interest (as assumed by many theories) but also by a basic human need he calls, "an inner sense of dignity." He believes that the desire for dignity – experiences of recognition, honor, respect, and pride, as individuals and as members of groups – is "a master concept" and the driving force of political events around the world.[2]

Fukuyama notes that many contemporary political movements share a core motivation: A group or nation is seeking to undo a feeling of humiliation and restore a feeling of dignity and pride. "In a wide variety of cases, a political leader has mobilized followers around the perception that a group's dignity has been affronted, disparaged, or otherwise disregarded." Fukuyama offers several examples of the demand for dignity: Vladimir Putin's effort to restore Russia as a great power; Hungary's Viktor Orban's effort "to regain our self-esteem"; China's Xi Jinping's effort to end "one hundred years of humiliation"; Osama Bin Laden's desire for revenge of the humiliation of Muslims and to "re-create the glories of an earlier Islamic civilization"; and Donald Trump's pledge to "make America great again." Fukuyama calls this, the politics of resentment.[3]

Economic conflicts, of course, have been a defining political issue in Western societies for centuries and are still important. Political parties in Western democracies have historically been organized by social class – a party of owners vs. a party of labor. Fukuyama believes that politics based on economic interests has given way to a politics based on demands for recognition; that our political attitudes are now motivated less by workers seeking higher pay and better working conditions, and more by workers wanting to be respected. Economic status and social respect are, of course, related. Higher pay is a sign of respect, but it is not the only one. Being listened to, feeling that your ideas and contributions are recognized and valued, are also expressions of respect.[4]

Several years ago, I attended a public interview with a retiring CEO of a major U.S. company. The CEO was asked about his negotiations with union representatives. The unions, he recalled, kept insisting that they wanted to be respected. The CEO, trained as an economist, left each meeting wondering, "what do they mean when they say they want to be respected, what tangible benefit are they asking for?" He then suddenly realized that what they meant was just what they said, "we want to be respected."

Political scientist Katherine Cramer spent several years talking with people in informal settings throughout the state of Wisconsin. Cramer spoke with people in diners, coffee shops, early morning gas station coffee klatches, and students in 4-H Clubs. She made an effort to meet with people of different ages, from different regions of the state, including many rural communities. In her conversations, Cramer learned that, in rural Wisconsin, feelings of both economic injustice (unfair taxes and government spending) and personal disrespect were important aspects of the political attitudes in these communities. Cramer also calls this, "the politics of resentment."

Cramer explains, "In a politics of resentment, we treat differences in political points of view as fundamental differences in who we are as human beings ... when we tell ourselves and others about how events have unfolded, the stories hinge on blaming our fellow citizens."[5] Cramer found that resentment increasingly dominated the attitudes of many people she spoke with. Wisconsinites, once "notoriously nice," had now become unfriendly. ("It's gotten downright nasty around here. People, in casual conversation, are treating each other like enemies." One man told another he had just met, "I don't talk to people like you.") Feelings of resentment and disrespect were also central to the political opinions of the Tea Party members Arlie Russell Hochschild interviewed in rural Louisiana.[6]

Our need for recognition takes both individual and collective forms. We seek recognition as individuals, based on our common humanity and the principle of universal human rights. The rights movements of the 20th and 21st centuries – civil rights for African Americans, women's rights, gay rights (and earlier, the abolition of slavery)-are based on this principle.

We also seek recognition and pride as members of groups. Ethnic and religious nationalism, supremacist ideologies, and anti-democratic, "populist" leaders appeal to these emotions. Extreme nationalist movements, past and present, offer feelings of "community, acceptance, and dignity... membership in a proud and ancient community and culture ...whose greatness will again be recognized"[7] (and, we should of course add, a scapegoat for their humiliation). White supremacists in the United States call themselves Proud Boys. This is the ominous, dark side of the need for honor and pride, responsible for some of the most monstrous events in human history.

The politics of humiliation

Philosopher Michael Sandel has presented a similar analysis to explain our current political polarization and discontent. Sandel agrees that we are motivated by a need for recognition – a feeling of appreciation and respect. He believes that this recognition is now denied to those in America without a college degree.

Sandel argues that political division in contemporary American society is based on a confluence of forces, partly economic but more fundamentally psychological. In our increasingly meritocratic and unequal society, white men without a college education have suffered more than a loss of job security and stagnant or declining wages; they have experienced a loss of "social esteem." In Sandel's analysis, our preoccupation with encouraging college education as the solution to the problems of working-class Americans, although well-intentioned, has unwittingly diminished the status of those who work at blue-collar jobs – workers who, in past generations, were more widely respected for their contributions to society and the prosperity that many of us enjoy. Lack of respect, at least as much as economic grievances, is the source of their resentment. Financial security matters, but feelings of pride matter more. Sandel calls this, the politics of humiliation.[8]

Anne Case and Angus Deaton, reporting their research on "deaths of despair," present a similar analysis.

"Many of the jobs that come with lower wages do not bring the sense of pride that can come with being part of a successful enterprise, even in a low-ranked position.... Workers, even in dangerous, dirty occupations ... could [in the past] be proud of their roles.... Jobs are not just a source of money; they are the basis for the rituals, customs, and routines of working-class life.... It is the loss of meaning, of dignity, of pride, and of self-respect ... that brings on despair, not just or even primarily the loss of money."[9]

Sandel notes that the politics of humiliation differ, in one important respect, from the politics of injustice. "Protest against injustice looks outward; it complains that the system is rigged, that the winners have cheated or manipulated their way to the top."[10] Humiliation adds to feelings of injustice, additional feelings of shame and self-doubt.

I believe that Fukuyama and Sandel are profoundly right in emphasizing the importance of dignity and pride in our current political polarization. Modern research on emotions supports this understanding. Feelings of pride and shame are a constant presence – a "master concept" – in our lives. Pride and shame (along with guilt and envy) are a special class of human emotions, often referred to as "self-conscious" or "self-evaluative" emotions.[11] We feel anxious or sad, for example, about events in the world. Pride and shame are different – we feel proud or ashamed of *ourselves*, especially how we feel about ourselves in the eyes of others.

We all need a feeling of pride. Our mental health depends on it, throughout life. We want (and need) to be respected – as individuals, in our families, and as members of a community. A feeling of social esteem allows us to engage confidently with others. We take pride in our ability to provide financial support for our families and to be role models for our children. If we do not find a feeling of pride in one area of life, we will look for it elsewhere.

In contrast, shame is one of the most painful human emotions. Shame is our instinctive response to failure, especially the public exposure of failure. Feelings of humiliation are one of the most destructive forces in our lives, in both personal and group psychology. As individuals, prolonged feelings of shame are deeply pathogenic, a cause of depression, substance abuse, suicide, abusive relationships of all kinds, and violence.[12]

Far more than other emotions, feelings of shame stay with us. We continue to remember past failures long after other emotions (for example, anxiety, sadness, or anger) have faded. Many of us can recall moments of embarrassment or humiliation, or when we failed to live up to our inner standards and ideals, from decades ago, that remain painful. Nations and ethnic groups memorialize historical events of national pride and humiliation for centuries.

Our indebtedness to others

Sandel argues that feelings of gratitude, belonging, and common purpose are necessary for a healthy and generous society. He writes,

> "...we cannot deliberate about common purposes and ends... without seeing ourselves as members of a community to which we are indebted. ... [Our meritocratic ethos] unraveled these moral ties.... [We are] less reliant on our fellow citizens, less grateful for the work they do, and less open to the claims of solidarity.... We are now in the midst of the angry whirlwind this unraveling has produced."[13]

Sandel quotes Robert F. Kennedy's understanding of this fundamental human need.

> "Essential values of our civilization [fellowship, community, patriotism] do not come from just buying and consuming goods together. They come instead from ... the kind of employment that lets a man say to his community, his family, his country, and, most important, to himself, 'I helped to build this country. I am a participant in its great public ventures.'"[14]

Kennedy's statement is an expression of the need for national pride in its positive form and may help us come closer together – to move away from a politics of resentment and grievance toward a politics of indebtedness (or, at least, to strengthen an awareness of indebtedness to counterbalance our grievances).

Let me offer a personal example. Over the last several years, I have had the opportunity to fly frequently to and from the newly renovated LaGuardia Airport in New York City. The airport is stunningly beautiful. I am reminded, each time I walk through the terminals, of the thousands of people of different occupations, at all levels of society, who made (and continue to make) this achievement possible – elected officials, business leaders, architects and builders, technology experts, transportation safety experts and workers, supervisors, lawyers, pilots and receptionists, maintenance workers, and many others – people who have come together to offer me, as a citizen, an experience of practical importance, aesthetic pleasure, and national pride that improves the quality of my life. I may still, from time to time (although not in my best moments) grumble about what seem to be unnecessary inconveniences or rudeness as I travel, but there is always a background feeling of gratitude, of belonging to a country that can come together to create this remarkable achievement of architecture and commerce.

I should feel the same gratitude every time I talk with a doctor and take medicine that improves the quality of my life. I am indebted not only to my doctor but also to biomedical researchers (at universities and in private industry) as well as medical technicians, medical entrepreneurs, nurses, and many others who have made my continued well-being possible.

RFK's vision ("I helped to build this country. I am a participant in its great public ventures") is an ideal shared by both liberals and conservatives, and a starting point for a shared pragmatic concern – how to restore a sense of "we-ness" in America – a society in which more people feel respected, a society with a stronger sense of belonging and community, a society that is less lonely,[15] and where more people have feelings of hope and pride.

How to achieve this society is a difficult problem and will require more than better dialogue; it may require new economic policies, improved education, and other social reforms. But the goals of a less divided society and greater national pride are shared by large numbers of Americans.[16] This is a place where we might find common ground, based on a universal human need.

The politics of fear

Philosopher Martha Nussbaum has presented a different understanding of the emotional causes of our current political polarization. Nussbaum believes that we are increasingly divided by fear.

Nussbaum contrasts emotions that bring people together – love, compassion, and hope – and those that separate us from others – fear, anger, disgust, and envy. In Nussbaum's analysis, fear is the most fundamental of these emotions. Anger, disgust, and envy are "children" of fear. These emotions and their expression in political attitudes (for example, racism, xenophobia, antisemitism, misogyny, and homophobia) are ultimately based on fear and draw their strength from fear.[17]

Nussbaum calls fear a "tyrant." Fear weakens compassion and contracts our circle of care and concern. Fear increases tribalism, both in its positive forms – providing safety and strengthening cooperation within the tribe – and its destructive forms – exclusion, hatred, and dehumanization of others. Fear increases support for authoritarianism[18] and erodes restraints on violence, cruelty, and revenge.[19]

Despite the instinctive nature of fear, Nussbaum argues that social and political attitudes based on fear are not "natural" or inevitable; they emerge under certain social conditions, often stoked by political leaders. Our fear comes both from the bottom up – as an instinctive reaction to others – and from the top down, abetted and cynically exploited by the dehumanizing rhetoric and explicit fear-mongering of politicians and media personalities.

Donald Trump's original and continuing message is fear. Tucker Carlson told his listeners that the Black Lives Matter movement "will come for you."[20] It is legitimate, of course, to criticize policies advocated by supporters of the Black Lives Matter movement. It is demagoguery to tell people that they "will come for you."

Fear (my way of life is endangered) and resentment ("they" are getting what I deserve) are an especially toxic mix.

Principles of constructive dialogue

Part II

From debate to dialogue

…neither the whole of truth nor the whole of good is revealed to any single observer, although each observer gains a partial superiority of insight from the particular position in which he stands.

William James, *On a Certain Blindness in Human Beings*

DOI: 10.4324/9781032679075-5

Is dialogue possible? **4**

Successful discussion of any important disagreement is based on a simple premise: We need to listen to each other. In both politics and our interpersonal relationships, there may be nothing as important and beneficial as patient and respectful listening. All the principles and recommendations in this book have a common goal – to improve the quality of our listening when talking with people who have different values and opinions on issues that matter to us.

But listening is difficult, especially in politics. Listening is difficult whenever we have strong feelings and strong opinions. Listening is difficult when we believe that our way of life is threatened or when the injustices we see and experience – the wrongs we want to right – evoke outrage and hatred. Listening is difficult (perhaps, impossible) when we have been insulted or disrespected, and in the absence of trust. In most political discussions, we are not really listening; we have already formed a judgment or an opinion. We are waiting for an opportunity to present our arguments and defend our side, looking for weaknesses to attack, not truths to acknowledge. We are not trying to learn more. New York Times columnist Jessica Grose recently described this attitude, citing the work of Consensus Building Institute, as "rebuttal mode."[1] In politics, rebuttal mode is our default setting – and our nemesis.

We have all experienced what happens when we are speaking, and someone is not listening. We become frustrated and angry. Our

DOI: 10.4324/9781032679075-6

voices get louder and more insistent. We exaggerate. We become stubborn and self-righteous, more certain that we are right and more intransigent in our demands. The longer we feel that we are not being heard, the angrier and more stubborn we are likely to become.

In healthy relationships – among friends, colleagues, and romantic partners, and between parents and children – we find ways to repair hurtful interactions – to apologize if we have been insensitive or neglectful and restore warmth and trust. When repair processes are unsuccessful, relationships become strained or break down. We may be unwilling to make the effort of repair, or we don't know how.

Over time, withdrawal, defensiveness, and blaming further erode our willingness to listen. We become "sensitized" – every criticism now feels like disrespect. Feelings of anger and unfairness are more easily evoked and more difficult to repair.

A vicious cyclone

In politics, as in our personal lives, when we feel that our needs and our grievances have not been heard or that we have been treated with disrespect, a vicious cycle is set in motion. Feelings of disrespect turn disagreement into resentment and contempt. These attitudes are then supported by partisan news outlets and on social media. We now see only extremism on the other side. We believe that our opponents are willfully blind to injustices and indignities we experience, that our values have been attacked, denigrated, or ignored, and that our way of life is "under siege." Psychologist Peter Coleman describes current American politics as a particularly malignant form of a vicious cycle he calls a "vicious cyclone," drawing more and more biased information and hateful feelings into its vortex.[2]

Now, in our polarized time (but to some extent always), when we hear a politician speak, the first question we ask ourselves is not about policies. We want to know, "Is he for me or for them?" How we feel about this basic question determines our emotional bias and our attitude toward everything that follows.

There is an antidote to this malignant process. Listening is possible, even in extreme circumstances. When we feel that someone has listened, the benefits are often immediate and sometimes profound. Listening leads to openness and "softening."[3] Listening begets listening, and empathy begets empathy.

Katherine Cramer asks, "If the people I spent time with [rural residents of Wisconsin] had perceived that policy makers had listened to [their] concerns before creating government programs, would they have felt differently about those programs?" She suggests that the answer is yes.

Listening is first an attitude, then a skill. If we are going to listen constructively and come closer together, we begin with a commitment to dignity and respect. We need, in some way, to feel – and our opponents must also feel – "affirmed." We need to hear our opponents' personal stories and learn about the experiences that were formative in the development of their attitudes and what is important to them now – the stresses, anxieties, and grievances of their lives, the injustices they experience, the values they try to live by, and the stories that inspire them.

When we listen, we begin with an attitude of wanting to know more. We make an effort to find what is true in what someone is saying, even if we can only find a kernel of truth. We look for an experience we can understand. We make a gesture of empathy and let them know that their feelings are understandable, even if we disagree.

Listening in this way allows us to engage in dialogue instead of debate. We should express our "opinions" less often and, instead, express our "concerns." We need to consider someone else's opinion with greater charity and regard our own with less certainty and more humility.

We need to acknowledge the limits of our political attitudes and ideology, to move away from false dichotomies, and work toward greater pragmatism. We need to think less often of "either/or" and "for/against," and more often of "how" and "and/also." These shifts – from debate to dialogue; from opinions to concerns; from certainty to humility; and from ideology to pragmatism – are often a new form of conversation and a game changer in both families and politics.

An "exhausted majority"

I need to briefly address several possible objections to the proposals I will present. To some readers, many of the concepts and recommendations I will discuss in the following chapters – affirmations, empathy, genuine openness, and dialogue – may seem like platitudes or common sense.

But they are not common practice. Psychologist Michael Mascolo analyzed a debate between two college professors on the issue of gun control. The debate consisted of ninety-one conversational turns. In ninety turns, each professor expressed an "adversarial position." Only *one statement* in this debate included "a mention of an interest, need, or problem" that was the source of the professor's beliefs. This is the most common form of political discussion, and it is exactly the wrong way for us to talk with each other.[4]

Some readers may feel that the possibility of working toward constructive dialogue with political opponents is naive or counterproductive. Politics, in this view, is not about feelings and ideas; politics is now (and has always been) about self-interest – a conflict between those with power and those without, between the haves (who justify their wealth and status with a political ideology) and the have-nots (who are seeking greater political influence, economic security, and an increasing share of society's wealth).[5] Political battles need to be fought; vested interests will give ground only when they have to; dialogue is a distraction, at best, a waste of time.

Some readers may believe that efforts at dialogue are naive for other reasons – that politics is less about ideology or economic self-interest than about culture; that our political differences are based on competing ideas about morality and society that are not open to discussion of any kind.[6] From this perspective, dialogue is no match for the intolerance, hatred, and antidemocratic forces on the extreme right or the self-righteous arrogance and intolerance of the extreme left.

Other readers may feel that we are coming apart as a society not because of different ideas and values but because of the facts of our daily lives. In this view, our society has become so divided, that we now live such separate lives, with vastly different resources and opportunities, that we will remain resentful and divided until economic and social conditions fundamentally change.

There is some truth in all these points of view. Motivations of power and self-interest, cultural fundamentalism, and increasingly unequal economic conditions all contribute to political polarization and limit the possibility of dialogue and understanding. I will also concede that some political opinions are beyond the pale of reasonable discussion and debate. In politics, our stated opinions (especially, the opinions of politicians) may camouflage other, socially unacceptable motivations (for example, racism) or are simply dishonest, based entirely on political expediency. Opinions presented as general principles may be hypocritical and quickly abandoned when political circumstances change. Many people in the political world have no interest in finding common ground; only immediate partisan advantage matters. The principles of constructive dialogue and reasoned argument I will describe are also unlikely to have any influence on extreme opinions encased in moral certainty and on those who believe in conspiracy theories; these beliefs are symptoms of a malignancy that is too far advanced for the remedies I can offer.

But opportunistic and hypocritical political attitudes, cynical politicians, self-interest rationalized as political philosophy, economic inequality, and irreconcilable cultural beliefs have always been present, and our contempt for our opponents has not always been this extreme. How we listen and talk with each other still matters. For many of us, improved dialogue and understanding are possible.

There is some hopefulness in surveys of American voters. A consensus has emerged among political scientists that "substantial swaths of American society (including many who identify as Democrat or Republican) are fed up with surging sectarianism." A 2018 survey by *More in Common* found that most Americans, both liberal and conservative, want our political parties to compromise more often. These voters have been labeled the "exhausted majority."[7]

There is also some hopefulness in the theories I reviewed and the synthesis I offered in the preceding chapters. Although we may have different temperaments and predispositions, different worldviews, visions of human nature, or moral foundations, very few of us are *always* tender-minded or tough-minded, empathic or strict, constrained or unconstrained, fixed or fluid in our ideas about society and our relationships with others. Most of us, in some aspect of our lives, recognize the need for both compassion and sources of authority; the need to end injustice and still preserve traditions and act in self-defense. There are limits to all political ideologies. Although we may believe in different political ideas, when confronted with real-world problems, ideology breaks down. (Political extremism and religious fundamentalism are exceptions to this statement.)

In the following chapters, I will describe fundamental principles of constructive dialogue and reasoned debate – alternatives and antidotes to the angry, repetitive, and unproductive arguments that now dominate our political culture.

A language of dignity and respect

5

Constructive dialogue requires a sustained effort to act toward others with dignity and respect. In political discussions, especially in our current political climate, this is easier said than done. Fortunately, there are now many programs, based on extensive experience and supported by research, that teach us how to do this more successfully, more often.

The principle of dignity has been persuasively articulated by Donna Hicks of the Harvard Weatherhead Center for International Affairs. Hicks has presented a "dignity model" for promoting dialogue and conflict resolution between opposing groups, derived from her experience mediating international conflicts in Israel-Palestine, Sri Lanka, Colombia, the United States – Cuba, and Northern Ireland. Hicks argues that progress toward a peaceful solution of long-standing conflicts depends on a single core principle. In Hicks' workshops and negotiations, successful conflict resolution begins with a commitment to dignity – and fails without it. When discussions and negotiations break down, the emotional undercurrent that has disrupted the reconciliation process is almost always an unacknowledged or unrepaired violation of dignity. Dignity violations are the elephant in the room.[1]

Our dignity is violated when we are ignored, slighted, or made to feel inferior, and when we are made to feel that our lives do not matter. Exclusion and ridicule are especially painful experiences

DOI: 10.4324/9781032679075-7

of indignity. Violations of dignity, whether obvious and intended, or subtle and unintentional, are an emotional injury that evokes feelings of shame and anger, defensiveness and withdrawal, and, often, a need to retaliate, in some form. Hicks notes that the pain caused by injuries to our dignity is equivalent to physical pain and processed in the same areas of the brain.

Hicks therefore believes that successful conflict resolution requires a "language of dignity" – an explicit affirmation of each person's dignity, an awareness of potential dignity violations, and a willingness to work toward repair of perceived violations of dignity when they occur.

Hicks emphasizes an important difference between dignity and respect. Dignity is a universal right, prior to respect; respect is earned. We respect others for their efforts, their accomplishments and character, and their contributions to their families and communities. We do not respect opponents who are bigoted, selfish, callous, or dishonest. Although we may not respect someone, they are still entitled to be regarded with dignity. This distinction is important and may help us begin to talk with people we don't respect.

A soldier and his victim

Hicks reports an inspiring and instructive encounter between Ronnie, a former IRA soldier, and Malcolm, a British police officer whom Ronnie had shot and almost killed several decades earlier. The meeting between Ronnie and Malcolm, organized as part of a BBC television series, *Facing the Truth*, included Hicks and Archbishop Desmond Tutu as facilitators.

In the meeting, both Ronnie and Malcolm tell their stories, uninterrupted. Ronnie describes the circumstances of his life and his reason for joining the IRA at age 16. He tells of his hopelessness and feeling shut out of any political process. He talks about seeing a friend killed by British police and knowing that joining the IRA would end, for him, "in the graveyard or in jail."

Malcolm, for the first time, talks about the events of the night Ronnie shot him. He tells Ronnie about his children – that if he had died that night, they would have grown up without a father – and that his youngest child would never have been born. He asks Ronnie if he has any children. He also tells Ronnie, "I think if I had been you, I would have done the same thing you did." After their conversation, Ronnie and Malcolm become friends.

The story of Ronnie and Malcolm is extraordinary in several ways. It is extraordinarily moving and inspirational; it may also be exceptional in its rarity. Although rare, this discussion illustrates several important elements of constructive dialogue.

The meeting between Ronnie and Malcolm required extensive preparation to establish a sufficient degree of trust. Hicks believes that the presence of a respected authority (in this case, Archbishop Tutu) to ensure the emotional safety and dignity of the participants is often a prerequisite for the success of these difficult conversations.

Malcolm allows Ronnie to tell his story, and he extends a remarkable gesture of empathy when he says, "If I had been you…" Malcolm then tells his story and implicitly challenges Ronnie to recognize *his* humanity – if he had died that night, his children would have grown up without a father. This is what I find so remarkable about this encounter. Malcolm expresses uncommon empathy for the man who shot him, then challenges him to feel and extend empathy in return.

There can be no doubt about the importance of dignity in our personal and civic lives. Human history offers far too many examples of unspeakable acts of indignity: The experience of African Americans throughout U.S. history, in language and action; the experience of indigenous peoples – Native Americans, the First Nations of Canada and Australia, of Blacks in South Africa, and of other colonized people; of Jews and other victims of genocide; of LGBTQ people and all dehumanized "others" – ethnic minorities around the world. Erik Erikson called this aspect of human nature, "pseudo-speciation."[2] We also experience indignity in less violent but still painful forms: being treated or spoken to as if we are inferior; being ignored or insulted; being denied a job or a mortgage because of our race, gender, or sexual orientation.

The mutual hostility of our current politics is often animated (and then justified) by perceived indignities on both sides.

A language of dignity in contemporary America

Our willingness and the effort we make to listen, to want to know more, and to repair unintended slights (often, with a simple apology) are affirmations of dignity and fundamental attitudes of constructive dialogue. When we make a commitment to dignity, we enter conversations with an attitude of "what can I learn from this person, what values and goals do we share, what can I affirm about her." Hicks reports that, in her workshops, a simple statement, "I know that this is important to you," is often sufficient to repair an emotional injury. (This is easy to forget during a political argument.) Deeper, more painful dignity violations are more difficult to repair and may require more extensive discussion and deeper apologies.

We affirm the dignity of our opponents when we respect and value the work that they do at their jobs or at home, their love and commitment to their families, and their contributions to their communities. We affirm the dignity of working-class Americans – preschool teachers and childcare workers, builders and maintenance workers, military personnel, and many others – by valuing their essential contributions to our lives and the health of our society (and, in my opinion, by rewarding them with much higher pay. This last opinion is pragmatic and debatable; the importance of dignity and respect are not.)

If we are discussing policing in America, we affirm the dignity of police officers when we recognize the daily demands and the danger of their work, and their dedication to their families and to our safety. We affirm the dignity of black Americans when we recognize the continuing presence of racism – the injustice of unequal treatment, of harsher punishments for the same offense, of many other forms of discrimination, and the tragedy of the loss of innocent lives. We affirm the dignity of Native Americans when we acknowledge the injustice and cruelty they have endured for centuries.

We affirm the dignity of pro-life advocates by recognizing the depth and sincerity of their religious beliefs and their deeply felt conviction that, from the moment of conception, a fetus is a life, and because it is a life, it must be protected. We affirm the dignity of pro-choice advocates by recognizing the depth and sincerity of their compassion and concern for the lives of women and their conviction that all women should be free to make personal medical choices. These affirmations of dignity will not resolve our differences; however, they open the possibility of more civil and respectful disagreement.

Value affirmations

The importance of feeling affirmed for our willingness to consider opposing opinions has been demonstrated in a series of studies conducted over more than two decades by social psychologist Geoffrey Cohen and his colleagues. In some of these experiments, participants are asked to write about personal values, unrelated to politics, that are a source of meaning in their lives. In other studies, participants receive positive feedback on their ability to be sensitive to the emotions of others. These exercises are called "value affirmations." Participants then read an article in opposition to their opinion on a political issue (for example, capital punishment). Those who had first received a value affirmation more often rated the article as reasonable and persuasive, and they became more moderate in their attitudes toward capital punishment, whether they supported or opposed it. Cohen concludes that a feeling of being affirmed is "a catalyst for opening peoples' minds."[3]

Cohen asks an important question: "How might we as individuals [in our daily lives] provide affirmation to those from across the political divide to build better relations and perhaps find common ground?" He recommends, based on his research, that "we can state our belief in shared values, such as family, the world the next generation of children will inherit, and caring for friends and community. We can ... ask people in a genuinely curious manner about what their views are and why they hold them - which helps to make people feel seen and heard. And we can listen respectfully to their answers."[4]

Cohen advises that we are more successful in fostering openness when we express our ideas not as incontrovertible facts or absolute truth, but instead, in more qualified and subjective (and therefore less confrontational) language, as our opinion. He calls this, "perspective-giving" as a complement to the more traditional concept of "perspective taking." I would take this recommendation even further; whenever possible, instead of expressing our opinions, we should express our "concerns." (I will discuss this recommendation in more detail in Chapter 9.)

This advice may seem self-evident, but, in real life, it is not. In most political conversations, we do not express opinions in the qualified way that Cohen recommends. Far more often, we express our opinions not as "perspectives" but as "positions"[5] or "pronouncements."[6]

The dehumanizing language now commonplace in American politics is one of the most disheartening and destructive aspects of our current political culture. We cannot change how politicians speak, except with our votes. But we can change how we speak to each other.

Learn someone's personal story   **6**

One of the best ways to begin a more constructive political discussion is to learn about someone's personal story (as Ronnie and Malcolm do). When we make an effort to get to know, in detail, about someone's life, we will almost always find some common experience or shared value, even with people whose opinions are antithetical to our own. If we want to understand someone's opinions, we should listen to their stories.[1]

We need to take the time to learn about the lives of people we disagree with, the experiences that were formative in the development of their opinions, and what is important to them now – the anxieties, frustrations, and struggles of their daily lives, the events that evoke their outrage, and the feelings that inspire them.

Stories have an emotional appeal and a truth value that ideas often lack. Stories are, to some extent, unarguable. We do not often change (or open) our minds when we are exposed to different opinions and ideas. Ideas begin with stories, and when we are uncertain about what to think, we instinctively return to the stories that are the source of our ideas.

All of us have families; we were all children; many of us are parents. Most of us have jobs or hobbies that require effort, discipline, or creativity, as well as some degree of anxiety, frustration, conflict, and stress (and, when we are fortunate, feelings of satisfaction and pride). We all know how it feels, at some point in our lives,

DOI: 10.4324/9781032679075-8

to feel that we have been treated unfairly; to be ignored, excluded, or disrespected; to feel that our effort has not been recognized or appreciated; or to feel that we don't belong.

Our interest and willingness to learn someone's personal story is an affirmation of dignity; we have communicated that her experience matters to us. If we listen to the stories of people's lives, we may still disagree. Listening to someone's story may not change our opinion about how to solve a problem. We may believe that what they have told us is not the whole story. But personal stories almost always humanize our opponent, and our hostility will be softened.

The point of listening to someone's story is not to approve or disapprove, but to allow ourselves to be influenced emotionally, to recognize, more deeply than we have before, that human problems are complex, and to move us away from oversimplification and certainty toward a better understanding of another person's values and concerns.[2]

Stories are the source of our sympathy or our outrage, our sense of unfairness and injustice. The stories of demagogues are intended to make us afraid (and they are often successful). Stories of heroic leaders are intended (and perhaps necessary) to strengthen a sense of common purpose and motivate collective effort. We tell stories to our children and to graduating students hoping to inspire them – stories of great and good women and men, what they have achieved and how they have helped us – to preserve our freedom, to help and sustain us, and to save our lives. If we have become cynical and don't tell these stories, we have deprived our children of an important source of motivation and feelings of pride.

Here are some of the many stories that animate our current political divide. Liberals and conservatives often tell different stories. But if we are willing to put aside our defensiveness, there are many stories we can all agree on. I have chosen these examples because each of these stories has had a personal effect on me. In some cases, the stories were inspiring and have remained important sources of my political beliefs; others were stories of unbearable grief and anger; other stories helped me see events from a new perspective, softening my prejudices against people I disagree with and helping me see that there is more than one side to every story.

"Deep stories" and our political beliefs Stories of resentment

Katherine Cramer's interviews with residents of Wisconsin, discussed in Chapter 3, are a model for how we should listen and talk with each other. Cramer's questions are consistently respectful but also probing and challenging. She begins by asking, "What are the big concerns here these days?" and "I want to learn more about how you think and feel." She expressed empathy for their frustrations, promised to return, and then kept her promise. (This was a new experience for many of the people she met; in rural areas, most residents expect that when people from the university come to town, they "pronounce what's good and then leave.")

In talking about their lives, the rural residents Cramer spoke with focused on their daily economic struggles, a feeling of resentment that their needs were not understood by those in state government, that their taxes were spent on less deserving others, and that they were not receiving their fair share of benefits from the taxes they paid. They were resentful about a perceived lack of power, lack of fairness, and lack of respect. They spoke often about how their lives were different from people who lived in Wisconsin's major cities of Madison and Milwaukee.

Cramer calls this "rural consciousness" – the feeling that "people like them, in places like theirs, were overlooked and disrespected." This is how people in rural Wisconsin saw politics – through the lens of rural consciousness.[3] Cramer learned that support for the Tea Party in rural Wisconsin is not based on a libertarian political philosophy; instead, it is based on a sense of injustice. The rural residents she spoke with wanted politicians to understand and respect the way rural folks live, their concerns and desires. They supported Scott Walker because "someone was finally acknowledging the injustice of their hard-earned money being shunted toward the undeserving."[4]

Sociologist Arlie Russell Hochschild also spent several years getting to know members of the Tea Party in rural Louisiana, listening to their political opinions and personal stories, attending their recitals and social events, and becoming friends. Hochschild begins with a concern about our increasing political divide. She wants to "learn how life *feels* to people on the right ... to understand... the emotion that underlies politics." As a liberal college professor from Berkeley, California, Hochschild knew that she needed to cross the empathy wall. "I had to imagine myself in their shoes."

Many of Hochschild's discussions focused on a "keyhole" issue of environmental regulation. She spoke with people whose lives and livelihoods had been severely impacted by industrial pollution. The area of Louisiana she visited is one of the most polluted in the country; oil and chemical companies had willfully and illegally dumped toxic chemical waste into local bayous. Fish, birds, and other animals that lived along the river died; residents were no longer able to safely swim and fish; both adults and children suffered higher rates of cancer. (Nine members of one of the families Hochschild spoke with developed different forms of cancer.) Drilling accidents created giant sinkholes that swallowed trees and houses and released toxic liquids and gases into the air and water, forcing many residents to leave their homes. People mourned the loss of their communities.

Despite these devastating consequences of industrial pollution, most of the residents Hochschild spoke with consistently supported candidates who opposed government regulation of the companies whose pollutants were spoiling their land, water, and health. Hochschild calls this "the great paradox" – great pollution and great resistance to regulating the polluters.

Thinking about what she learned from her time in Louisiana, Hochschild came to understand that political attitudes (for all of us, she believes) are based on a "deep story." Our deep story is the emotional foundation of our political loyalties. To understand the people she met in Louisiana, Hochschild composed a composite deep story that expressed "...the emotions that were the source of their political beliefs: the hopes, fears, pride, shame, resentment, and anxiety in the lives of those I talked to."[5]

The story that Hochschild developed included all these feelings, but resentment had a central place. In this story, these Louisianans have been waiting in line for a chance to achieve the American Dream – a dream of progress toward a more secure and prosperous life than was possible for their parents and grandparents. They had worked hard and shown good moral character, and they had sacrificed for their family, church, and community. But the line isn't moving; they haven't gotten a raise in years and do not expect one soon. All around them, they see others being given preferential treatment - blacks (through affirmative action, welfare payments, or free lunches), immigrants, women, and overpaid public sector employees (most of whom are black and women) with cushy jobs, pensions, and tenure. These other groups are cutting in line. The Democratic Party has sympathy for the others (and not for them). Democrats are on the other side. They wonder why, causing suspicion and mistrust.

The deep story is about respect, a desire to feel seen and honored. Many of the people Hochschild spoke with do not feel respected; instead, they feel insulted. The deep story is also about cultural values – pride in the acceptance of hardship, not feeling like a victim or a "poor me." Feeling like a victim is anathema to the rural Louisianan attitude toward life.

When Hochschild finished writing the deep story, she sent it to her Tea Party friends to see if she had gotten it right, and they generally agreed that she had. Some of her friends told her that she needed to add other resentments – that "we are paying taxes that go to them," that "we want to feel proud to be an American, to say 'under god' when you salute the flag," and "we want a society that believes in clean, normal family life." To understand MAGA America, we need to listen to these stories.

Stories of patriotism

Francis Fukuyama argues that healthy societies offer their citizens "stories of peoplehood." Fukuyama believes that we need these stories. We need stories that allow us to celebrate our diverse individual identities but also strengthen feelings of patriotism and national pride.

Political scientist Steven Smith has also argued for the importance of patriotism, now out of fashion on many liberal college campuses. Smith presents a case for "patriotism - not nationalism - as the most fundamental political virtue." He distinguishes patriotism from nationalism on the right and cosmopolitanism on the left. An "enlightened patriotism" finds a middle course between these extremes.

Smith explains that the feeling of patriotism is like the love we have for our families. I love my family not because it is better than yours, but because it is *my* family. I feel gratitude and loyalty to my family because, although imperfect, they have loved me and helped me thrive. Smith offers this example: "I may feel an affinity for France's language, its food, its countryside, and its culture, but I can never love France the way a French person does. I can never feel the way a French woman feels when she hears La Marseillaise."[6] (And, of course, a French person cannot feel what I feel when I hear Ray Charles sing America the Beautiful or any moving rendition of the Star-Spangled Banner.)

There are many stories of American patriotism, beginning with our original patriots of the American Revolution. The eloquence of Jefferson's Declaration of Independence and Lincoln's Gettysburg Address are among our most inspiring expressions of American patriotism. In the present, we need to respect the patriotism of our military men and women and their willingness to risk their lives for our safety and freedom, even when we disagree with the mission they are sent to fight. Every person who serves in our armed forces is a patriot and deserves our respect. When we see them in airports, train stations, or on the street, we should remember to tell them, "Thank you for your service."

Everyone who serves in AmeriCorps, Teach for America, and the Peace Corps are patriots who are serving America and supporting our democracy. Our public-school teachers; our doctors, nurses, and other medical staff; our prosecuting attorneys and public defenders; our firefighters and the vast majority of our police officers are modern patriots who, along with many others, are also strengthening our country, keeping us safe, and helping us thrive. All these patriotic Americans also deserve our respect.

Stories of disillusionment

In her memoir, *An Unlikely Conservative*, Linda Chavez recounts her harrowing experiences, including physical threats, from radical leftists in the late 1960s and her disillusionment with the excesses of early affirmative action programs as a source of her turn toward conservatism.[7] Many other writers have offered stories that explained their conversion from liberalism to conservativism (or, less often, away from conservatism toward liberalism). Disillusionment is a central feature of almost all these stories.

More recently, New York Times columnist David French has described painful personal experiences of both regret and disillusionment. French was raised in a fundamentalist Christian community and remains a pro-life evangelical Christian. He began his career as a lawyer committed to socially conservative causes and attacking liberal policies and ideas. French served in Iraq as a JAG in 2007–2008 and witnessed the horrors of Islamic radicalism, seeing videos of beheadings with people cheering; "recruiting" women to become suicide bombers by raping them and then shaming them; and the murder of infants and mothers. When he returned home, he felt ashamed that, in his partisan writing, he had previously equated the danger of this evil abroad with the danger of liberalism in America.

Then, beginning in 2015, French began writing articles critical of Donald Trump. He especially criticized Trump's immorality and questioned his fitness to be President. He saw friends and acquaintances succumb to the birther conspiracy and "MAGA fever," a belief that Trump, despite his obvious moral failings, is "God's appointed leader."[8]

In response to his critique of Trump, French received hundreds of vicious, overtly racist personal attacks on his family (French's youngest daughter is black, adopted from Ethiopia) by the alt-right, and he learned of similar attacks on many other families. He was especially disillusioned by the tolerance of this despicable behavior by mainstream conservatives. As a result of his disillusionment, French did not change his core values and religious beliefs. Instead, these experiences left him "a man without a party."

Chavez's memoir and French's brief autobiographical introduction stand out from many others for their thoughtful account of the emotional conflict – and emotional toll – of their disillusionment.

Stories of injustice and grief

There are many, many more American stories. We all need to learn and recall the stories of the civil rights movement, of the indignity and violence endured by black Americans in the effort to end segregation and discrimination, and the more recent stories of Travon Martin, Philando Castile, George Floyd, Alton Sterling, Eric Garner, and Ahmaud Arbery. Whether we are liberal or conservative, we can all agree that these events should never happen. No one should be killed while innocently walking home from a store, driving, or jogging. We need to hear the stories of all victims of hate crimes.

There are the stories of Columbine and Sandy Hook, of Marjory Stoneman Douglas High School, of Uvalde and Las Vegas, the Pulse nightclub in Orlando, the Tree of Life Synagogue in Pittsburgh, the Emanuel African Methodist Episcopal Church in South Carolina, and the Covenant School in Nashville (and many more).

On July 7, 2016, five Dallas police officers were assassinated during a peaceful protest of the recent police shootings of Alton Sterling in Louisiana and Philando Castile in Minnesota. President Obama delivered a eulogy at the memorial service for these officers. He told a personal story of each officer. He told us how they had begun their day the morning they were killed. He spoke about their families, their dedication, and their service to others, risking their lives, every day, for our safety, regardless of race or political beliefs. He spoke of the depth of our shared sadness and outrage at this violence.

Obama continued with an acknowledgment of progress toward racial justice in America over the last half-century and his belief that the murders of these officers were not motivated by the values of the protesters but by perversion of their values. He then told the stories of the lives of innocent black men killed by police.

Obama's eulogy was praised by both liberals and conservatives. Conservatives were more qualified in their praise, acknowledging Obama's empathy and eloquence when talking about the lives of the murdered officers, then criticizing the length of the speech or the appropriateness of the occasion for talking about racial injustice. I have cited this speech because it is the best example I know of a politician telling both sides of an important story in contemporary America.[9]

Empathy and moral imagination 7

In Chapter 2, I argued that empathy, expressed in different ways – as feelings of compassion, an abhorrence of cruelty, and a wider circle of concern – is the core of a liberal worldview and a liberal political philosophy. I added, however, several important caveats: Liberals are not always empathic, conservatives are not always callous, and policies animated by empathy are not always wise. The importance of empathy to liberalism also does not mean that, in the midst of a political argument, liberals will always (or even usually) be empathic toward their opponents. Liberals are not immune from arrogance, one-sidedness, and ideological certainty – serious (and sometimes fatal) impediments to constructive discussion and finding common ground.

I am writing now about empathy in a related, but somewhat different sense. I will discuss empathy as a basic human need and a catalyst, perhaps a necessary precondition, for dialogue and mutual understanding, regardless of our political beliefs.

Empathy is an instinctive, unconscious emotional response to the feelings of others. It is also a conscious choice – a deliberate and often difficult effort to suspend judgment, to hear another person's story, to imagine ourselves in similar life circumstances, and to see (and feel) the world from their point of view. Empathy, journalist Jennifer Finney Boylan reminds us, is an act of "moral

DOI: 10.4324/9781032679075-9

imagination."[1] We can choose to feel – or turn away – from someone else's joy and pain.

We all know about the importance of empathy in our personal lives. Expressions of empathy – among friends, colleagues, spouses, parents, or children – have profound benefits for the quality of our relationships and our emotional health. When someone has expressed empathy, even the simple statement, "I know how you feel," we almost always feel better. Our disappointment and sadness now feel less painful, and we feel less alone.

Empathy is not only about feeling someone's sadness or pain; empathy also allows us to experience and share their joys.[2] A parent's empathy, for example, is present not only when we comfort a crying child. Empathy is present in our playfulness, when we intuitively sense a child's pleasure and have fun with her, when we respond with animated interest to children's expressions of curiosity and interest, with enthusiasm to their enthusiasm, and when we return their smiles with smiles of our own.

For the developing child, empathy is much more than a momentary feeling of comfort and understanding. Empathy is an essential nutrient of emotional development and social maturity, necessary for emotional health in childhood and for successful interpersonal relationships throughout life. Psychoanalysts often compare empathy to oxygen, and this is a useful analogy. Without enough oxygen, we begin to experience physical symptoms (often without knowing the cause). When empathy has eroded, in any relationship, at any time in our lives, we also experience symptoms. When we anticipate a judgmental or denigrating response from others, or when our feelings are met with indifference or scorn, we become more self-protective, in different ways – angry and resentful, or withdrawn and insecure.

Psychologist and neuroscientist Jamil Zaki reminds us that although empathy is a human instinct, it is not an immutable trait. We are not like Star Trek characters, either semi-human "empaths" who absorb the injuries and feelings of people around them or androids programmed without the capacity for empathy. In real life, we can become more open to others or more self-protective.[3] A critical question for political understanding is, "What are the social conditions that expand or erode empathy and compassion in our social and political lives?" How can we cross the empathy wall?

Empathy can be nurtured through early education[4] and through other experiences that deepen our feeling of connection with others (for example, working, singing, and praying together). Getting to know others whose life circumstances are different from our own, even reading stories about others, helps us understand more clearly what we have in common, to feel our common humanity more deeply.

Empathy, however, is fragile. Empathy can easily be eroded, partially or completely.[5] A feeling of being threatened may destroy empathy for others outside our group. Denigration and disrespect also limit our empathy. Abusive treatment as a child inhibits (and may completely prevent) the development of empathy.[6] Leaders in pursuit of greatness or revenge have little or no empathy for their opponents; the lives of individuals no longer matter, only the "greatness" of their nation.

Empathy can help us find common ground. When we are empathic, in any conversation or relationship, in politics and in our personal lives, we listen in a different way. When we listen with empathy, *we allow ourselves to be influenced* by someone else's feelings. (This is why empathy is essential for a successful marriage.)

Constructive discussion of any disagreement begins with a "gesture of empathy."[7] We make a gesture of empathy when we let someone know that we understand their feelings and concerns, even when we disagree. (Empathy does not mean agreement. This is a common misunderstanding of empathy, in both families and politics.) A gesture of empathy may not change someone's mind (or our own) on important issues, but it changes the tone of our disagreement, sometimes in a subtle, but still noticeable, way. Even small gestures of empathy convey a willingness to listen that almost always leads to some softening of our defensiveness and the harshness of our judgments, on both sides.[8]

Critics of empathy

There are some critics of empathy. In a provocative book, psychologist Paul Bloom challenged the conventional wisdom that "the problems we face as a society and as individuals are …due to a lack of empathy." Bloom argues, instead, that, "they are often due to too much of it." Although Bloom acknowledges some benefits of empathy, he concludes that, "on balance, empathy is a negative in human affairs" and "from a moral standpoint, we're better off without it."[9]

Bloom believes that decisions based on empathy will often be misguided, focusing our attention and resources on emotionally evocative individual stories in the here and now, but missing more long-term problems; that we are more likely to feel empathy for people who are similar rather than different from us; and that empathy often overwhelms rational decision-making. Bloom argues that when faced with moral problems, instead of empathy, we need the qualities of calmness and self-control, and a more diffuse kindness he calls, "rational compassion" – that we should use our heads rather than our hearts.

This is a false dichotomy. Empathy should inform and influence, but not determine, our opinions and actions. We can be both empathic and objective. We can use both our head and our heart. The importance of empathy for coming closer together does not mean that our political opinions should be decided only on the basis of empathy and that we should all become liberals. Empathy offers one perspective; there are always other, competing perspectives and concerns. In politics (as in parenting) an empathic response is not always the right response. Parents can (and often should) feel empathy for a child's disappointment and still say no.

Bloom argues that empathy focuses our attention on the distress of single individuals, neglecting the suffering of many others. This is a misunderstanding of empathy. From the suffering of one person, we often generalize to the suffering of others, from one suffering animal to other suffering animals,[10] from one person living with HIV to others with HIV,[11] and from one child to other children. The critics are wrong. We are not better off without empathy; on the contrary, empathy enriches us, immeasurably.

Moral imagination in contemporary America

In their eulogies for police officers killed in Dallas, Texas, in July 2016, Presidents George W. Bush and Barack Obama spoke about the importance of empathy for bridging our national divide.

President Bush said,

> At our best, we practice empathy, imagining ourselves in the lives and circumstances of others. This is the bridge across our nation's deepest divisions. And it is not merely a matter of tolerance, but of learning from the struggles and stories of our fellow citizens and finding our better selves in the process.[12]

President Obama said,

> ...with an open heart, we can learn to stand in each other's shoes and look at the world through each other's eyes, so that maybe the police officer sees his own son in that teenager with a hoodie who's kind of goofing off but not dangerous - and the teenager - maybe the teenager will see in the police officer the same words and values and authority of his parents.[13]

I have not heard any statements from political leaders that convey the essence and importance of empathy with greater insight and clarity.

In 2021, Utah Governor Spencer Cox, a Republican, vetoed a bill, passed by his own party, banning transgender girls from playing in female sports. Cox explained his opposition to the bill (as reported by ABC4 News):

> "If you have not spent time with transgender youth, then I would encourage you to pause on this issue...We have so many people who are in a very difficult spot right now. And we have very few, if any, transgender girls participating in sports ...When you spend time with these kids, it changes your heart in important ways...These kids are, they are just trying to stay alive. You know, there is a reason none of them are playing

sports...And so, I just think there is a better way, and I hope that there will be enough grace in our state to find a better solution."... "I don't understand all of this; I don't, but I'm trying to understand more, I'm trying to listen and learn, and again trying to help kids figure out who they are, and to keep them alive."[14]

Governor Cox's statements illustrate many of the principles of constructive dialogue I will discuss. He took the time to listen, to hear these children's stories, and to understand their concerns. He listened with an attitude of openness ("I'm trying to listen and learn"). He was willing to acknowledge his uncertainty and seek a better solution even if he didn't, at that moment, know what the solution would be. And he had the courage to oppose the majority of his party, most of whom seemed to regard transgender kids as a threat or as seeking an unfair advantage. Governor Cox listened with empathy and changed his heart. Other elected officials, however, have not shown the same capacity for empathy and moral imagination. Sadly, Governor Cox is an exception.

Republican Senator Rob Portman, an opponent of gay marriage, changed his position on marriage equality after his son came out as gay. Senator Portman offered a moving statement of love and support for his son. He explained that discussions with colleagues, members of his church community, and personal reflections on biblical teaching "allowed me to think of this issue from a new perspective."

Senator Portman's support for gay marriage is, at the same time, both encouraging and disheartening. It is always encouraging when a person in public life is willing to learn from someone else's experience and change their mind. But it is also disheartening. Why didn't Senator Portman take the time to have a conversation (or, even better, a dialogue, as I will discuss in Chapter 8) with advocates for gay marriage *before* he learned that his son was gay? Why didn't he feel that getting to know gay people would be helpful or necessary for coming to an opinion on the issue of marriage equality? Senator Portman's later empathy is a welcome repair of his earlier failure of moral imagination.

Following the killing of eighteen people in Lewiston, Maine, in October 2023, Democratic Congressman Jared Golden, who represents the congressional district that includes Lewiston, announced that he had reversed his opposition to gun control legislation. Congressman Golden now supports a ban on assault rifles like the one used in this shooting. The congressman asked for "forgiveness and support as I seek to put an end to these terrible shootings."

Like Senator Portman's change of heart, Congressman Goldin's announcement reflects a failure of moral imagination. A mass shooting had occurred in *his* district, and he now supports an assault weapons ban. But the murder of twenty-six first graders and teachers at Sandy Hook Elementary School ten years earlier apparently did not change his mind, nor did so many other mass shootings. I would like to ask Congressman Golden if, in the public and private debates that took place during his time in Congress, he ever met with representatives of Sandy Hook Promise, an organization of parents of children killed in Newtown, Connecticut, dedicated to reducing gun violence. Personally, I am glad that Congressman Golden changed his mind, but I am dismayed by his prior failure of moral imagination.

Crossing the empathy wall

Here are some suggestions for how we might be able, more often, to cross the empathy wall.

Imagine that you are the husband, wife, or child of a police officer killed while protecting the public. Or that you are a farmer or small business owner, faced with increasing costs of taxes, payroll, and safety regulations, struggling to stay in business.

Imagine that you are the parent of a teenage boy walking innocently home from the store, confronted by an armed private security guard. Or that you are jogging near your home, murdered by people you do not know, who hate you because of your race. Or that you are the parent of a 12-year-old boy shot by a police officer while playing with a toy pistol in a park. Or the victim of any hate crime.

If you are pro-choice or pro-marriage equality, it is still possible, without changing your beliefs, to imagine how someone raised in a conservative religious family would need time – or may never be able – to accept these ideas. Or imagine someone who sees a sonogram of a developing fetus and experiences a spiritual awakening to the miracle of life, a feeling that evokes a conviction that destroying this developing life is wrong – not only the wrong choice for her but morally wrong.

If you are pro-life, it is still possible to imagine the despair of a teenage girl who becomes pregnant or the sadness and anguish of a woman whose health is threatened by pregnancy, and still maintain (but soften) your opposition to abortion.

If you were reading any of the examples in this chapter and said to yourself, "Yes, but…" I will offer some advice. Before you say, "but," take more time. Allow yourself to be influenced by another person's experience or feelings. You may not change your opinion, but that's not the point. In counseling with couples, spouses are often instructed not to use the word "but." Saying "but" is like pressing the delete key on everything that had just been said.

This is important advice, although difficult to follow, in personal relationships and in politics: Instead of saying, "but," say "and."

From debate to dialogue   **8**

When we make a sustained effort to regard our opponents with dignity and respect, when we listen to their personal stories and tell them our own, and when we make a conscious effort to see and feel about the world the way they do, we have taken several steps away from unproductive argument toward a new form of discussion. We have begun a dialogue.

Dialogue is much more than a civil and respectful exchange of ideas. Dialogue is an uncommon and qualitatively different kind of conversation. Based on extensive experience in public opinion research and facilitating intergroup relations, Daniel Yankelovich offered a model for resolving group conflicts he called, "the magic of dialogue."[1]

A dialogue is not a negotiation or a problem-solving discussion (although it may lead to problem-solving). In a dialogue, we are listening with "genuine openness of each to the concerns of the other." In a dialogue, each person is trying to learn more about why someone feels and thinks the way they do.

Debate is the opposite of dialogue. The purpose of debate is to win an argument. In a debate, we assume that there is a right answer (and I have it). In a dialogue, we assume that many people have pieces of the answer and that together we are more likely to find a solution. Debates consist primarily of an "exchange of adversarial positions." Dialogue is about reexamining all positions and

DOI: 10.4324/9781032679075-10

exploring common ground. In a dialogue, we acknowledge that someone else's thinking may improve our own. We are looking to discover new options rather than trying to change someone's mind. Yankelovich explains, "You can't win or lose a dialogue."

In political discussions, we may think that we are having a dialogue, but we are still having a debate. Even brief moments of dialogue, however, can make a difference, changing the tone of subsequent discussion and debate.

Successful dialogue has profound benefits for all participants. Dialogue transforms "transactions" into "relationships." The benefits of dialogue are both tangible – reducing conflict and establishing a foundation for future problem-solving – and intangible – creating a deeper feeling of emotional connection and increased trust. For most of us, as citizens and in our family relationships, the intangible benefits may be the most important.

It is tempting, in our highly polarized time, to dismiss the magic of dialogue as naive and impractical, to assume that we cannot come close to the goal of genuine openness in our current state of mutual mistrust and contempt. A skeptic is also likely to ask, is dialogue really magic?

This skepticism may be valid, up to a point. Dialogue is difficult, requiring willingness, effort, and discipline. How often, even in respectful conversations, do we make a sustained effort to listen with empathy and search for value in someone else's ideas? The temptation to debate is sometimes impossible to resist.

But I believe that Yankelovich is right, even profoundly right. In therapeutic work with families, dialogue has the same benefits, both tangible and intangible, that Yankelovich describes in business and politics. I have repeatedly seen moments of dialogue help families get unstuck from stubborn conflicts, at times when spouses, parents, and children have almost given up and given in to pessimism and despair.

Moments of dialogue often produce a noticeable, and sometimes tearful, softening of feelings. In these moments, we have an opportunity to set in motion a fulcrum shift in family relationships – a movement away from frequent criticism, anger, and emotional withdrawal and toward renewed feelings of warmth, appreciation, and pride. Moments of dialogue, especially when followed by small changes of attitude or behavior, help turn troubled family relationships around.

In most political conversations, despite its many benefits, dialogue is only a first step – a necessary but not sufficient condition for coming closer together. We still need to debate. We still need to challenge our opponents, to point out facts they are not aware of, consequences they may not have considered, and reasons (for or against) they have not thought of. If we don't respectfully question and challenge others, we lose an opportunity to understand their deeper concerns.

But moments of dialogue change the nature of the debate. During a dialogue, we allow ourselves to be influenced, in some way, by another person's feelings, an essential condition for all successful relationships. When this happens, it is close to magic.

Strategic optimism

Psychologist Herbert Kelman, who spent a long and distinguished career working to resolve intractable international conflicts, presented the concept of "strategic optimism" as a principle of peaceful conflict resolution. Kelman explained that strategic optimism is not naive optimism. Strategic optimism is "not an unrealistic denial of malignant trends, but ... a deliberate strategy to promote change by actively searching for and accentuating whatever realistic possibilities for peaceful resolution of the conflict might be on the horizon."[2]

I was drawn to the idea of strategic optimism because this way of listening is also a principle of therapeutic change in working with troubled families. Too often, both in therapy and in politics, we focus our attention on trying to ameliorate malignant trends. (In family relationships, persistent feelings of shame and discouragement, pessimistic beliefs, frequent coercive interactions, and harsh or persistent criticism are malignant trends.) Identifying malignant interpersonal processes is often necessary, but it is not enough. It is equally important for therapists to *find and strengthen what is positive and hopeful* in family interactions. Successful child, adolescent, and family therapy often depends on this critical therapeutic skill.

Most families, even when there is frequent argument and strife, also have moments of warmth and emotional support. Children who are oppositional or defiant are not always uncooperative; there are also moments when they are considerate and kind. Children who have been angry and stubborn often make gestures of repair. Children whose parents believe that they are "lazy" or "selfish" show initiative and engagement in some projects and tasks, and genuine concern for others.

These positive behaviors are often buried (and, at times, further obscured by diagnostic labels). Parents, and sometimes children, may be dismissive of hopeful trends. A parent may overlook a child's kindness and effort, seeing, instead, only instances of rudeness, defiance, or withdrawal. Therapy with families offers an opportunity to recognize hopeful moments and build on them. Political arguments, like family conflicts, may also obscure the presence of hopeful moments, for example, the presence of shared values, concerns, and goals.

The practice of hope

Martha Nussbaum has presented a similar idea she calls, "the practice of hope." Nussbaum offers hope as an antidote to fear. She explains that hope is a practice, not just a feeling. Fear leads to some form of withdrawal (for example, cynicism, apathy, or despair) or a desire for revenge. Hope leads to active engagement in solving problems. "Hope expands and surges forward, fear shrinks back. Hope is vulnerable, fear self-protective."[3]

To practice hope, we need the support of a "hope-building and hope-sustaining community." Hope is difficult to sustain "in solitude." When we practice hope, we will still feel destructive emotions – fear, anger, disgust, envy, and a desire for revenge – but we are less likely to be overcome or "captured" by them.[4] This is the first sense in which hope is an antidote to fear.

Nussbaum offers several recommendations for involvement in activities that foster greater appreciation of our common humanity and strengthen hope. She cites evidence that the best antidote to fear of others is integration – to share our daily life with people who are, in some way, different from ourselves. This theory was originally proposed by psychologist Gordon Allport in his classic book, *The Nature of Prejudice.*[5] Allport's hypothesis has been extensively studied and confirmed, but also refined. Contact with others promotes greater tolerance and acceptance in most situations, but not all.[6]

A compelling example of this process is the transformation of attitudes of most Americans toward gay people since the 1960s. In 1966, *Time* magazine wrote that homosexuality was "a pernicious sickness," "a pathetic little second-rate substitute for reality, a pitiable flight from life."[7] Now, most of us have gotten to know someone who is gay, in person or on television. Just as Allport would have predicted, a remarkable social change has taken place. (I think of this as the *Will and Grace* theory of acceptance of gay rights.)[8]

Nussbaum also recommends literature, music, art, and religion (especially, participation in a religious community) as examples of the practice of hope and antidotes to fear of others. She believes that reading poetry and fiction, and singing, dancing, and acting in plays together help us experience others as "infinitely complex" people and promotes a sense of common work and joy. She also argues that engagement in non-violent protest movements is a form of hope, with Martin Luther King, Jr. as an inspiration. Dr. King's "I Have a Dream" speech is America's most eloquent and inspiring modern expression of hope.[9]

Work, sing, and pray with people you disagree with

Several scholars have proposed required national service, military or civilian, as an antidote to our current polarization and mutual contempt. Many of the writers whose work I discuss in this book, including Francis Fukuyama, Martha Nussbaum, Greg Lukianoff and Jonathan Haidt, Michael Sandel, Nicholas Kristof and Sheryl WuDunn, as well as Robert Reich and David Brooks, have endorsed this idea.

Rutgers University president Jonathan Holloway has written a persuasive article summarizing the benefits of national service for all young people. Holloway argues that national service would "support underserved urban and rural communities, help eliminate food deserts, contribute to rebuilding the nation's infrastructure, enrich our arts and culture, and bolster our community health clinics, classrooms, and preschools." National service would also "force all of our young people to better know one another, creating the opportunities to learn about and appreciate our differences... build bridges between people and turn them into citizens...change a life...open a mind and...save a democracy." [10]

Martha Nussbaum, Michael Sandel, and Robert Reich add an additional benefit, that national service will strengthen feelings of gratitude and a sense of responsibility for the common good. Nussbaum believes that we need to instill in our children "the idea that we owe our country some of our work and our time." Like Holloway, Nussbaum recommends that we should "send them to do the work that urgently needs doing all over America ... to see diversity of people in their country...and know the country in a new way." [11]

If possible, join a choir or religious group that includes people you disagree with. There is important recent research on the benefits of singing in a choir for both group cohesion and physical health. Singing together creates a feeling of closeness with others, increases our pain threshold, and may also make us more generous. [12] We derive similar benefits from praying together with people of different backgrounds. [13] It is difficult to hate someone you have sung next to in a choir or worked next to when building a house or as part of a medical team.

As an example of coming together through singing, I recommend *The Greatest Night in Pop*, a documentary film about the 1985 recording of *We Are the World*, written by Michael Jackson and Lionel Richie, to raise money to fight famine in Africa and recorded by what is probably the best group of popular singers ever assembled, including Ray Charles, Bob Dylan, Stevie Wonder, Bruce Springsteen, Dionne Warwick, Diana Ross, Cyndi Lauper, Paul Simon, and many more. In the film, we see how each singer retains his or her individual style but also needs to subordinate themselves to a common goal. (This may be especially difficult for a group of artistic superstars. Quincy Jones, who conducted the recording, posted a notice to all the singers: "Leave your ego at the door.") The result is a moving anthem to compassion, giving, and hope.

Principles of reasoned argument

Part III

From ideology to pragmatism

For where is the man that has incontestable evidence of the truth of all that he holds, or of the falsehood of all he condemns; or can say, that he has examined to the bottom all his own or other men's opinions? The necessity of believing without knowledge, nay, often upon very slight grounds, in this fleeting state of action and blindness we are in, should make us more busy and careful to inform ourselves than to constrain others... There is reason to think, that if men were better instructed themselves, they would be less imposing on others.

John Locke, *Essay Concerning Human Understanding*

DOI: 10.4324/9781032679075-11

From opinions to concerns

9

Political discussions are almost always framed as a choice between opposing opinions. We are asked (or ask ourselves) whether we agree or disagree with someone's opinion, proposed policy, or course of action. Of course, we are entitled to our opinions. It is also true, however, that we form our opinions too quickly and cling to them too stubbornly.

Especially in our mistrustful and polarized society, expressing an opinion, even when we support our ideas with logic and evidence, rarely changes anyone's mind or helps us find common ground. If our goal is to have a constructive discussion, it is far more important to understand someone's *concerns*. And then, in response, to express our concerns.

Emotionally and logically, concerns precede opinions. Once we have formed an opinion, some degree of hardening has already taken place. An opinion is a conclusion. When we debate opinions, we are beginning at (what should be) the end.

This principle is more than a semantic difference. Statements of concerns begin to transform an *ideological* disagreement into a *pragmatic* disagreement. Our differences are now more likely to be about priorities, not principles, about means rather than ends, and we are less likely to confuse means and ends. (Government spending, for example, whether social or military, is a means, not an end; the end is a productive and fair society or improved national security.)

DOI: 10.4324/9781032679075-12

The solution to a discussion of concerns is more likely to be "both/ and" instead of "either/or." This simple shift – from opinions to concerns – allows a much more successful discussion, in both family relationships and politics. It is now a new ball game – a different kind of conversation for families and for political opponents.

When we discuss issues in this way, we may find that, although we disagree about the causes of problems or what to do about them, we often share concerns. Or we may not share a concern, at least not to the same degree. But most concerns are likely to be *understandable*, a concern that we might share *in some circumstances*.

In political discussions, liberals are more likely to express empathic and humanitarian concerns – a concern about suffering, hardship, or injustice. Conservatives are likely to begin with concerns about maintaining traditions and existing institutions, a perceived threat to our security, or a concern about costs or regulations that may undermine initiative and productivity. In a discussion of concerns, we may still disagree. We may disagree on what constitutes injustice, we may disagree on priorities, and we will disagree on how a problem should be solved. But, again, our concerns are likely to be understandable, at least to some degree, and our disagreements are therefore less likely to evoke hatred and contempt. Most liberals can understand a conservative's concern with national security or the cost of entitlement spending. Most conservatives can understand a liberal's concern with alleviating poverty and ending discrimination. A conversation about concerns is different than a conversation about opinions. We debate opinions; we discuss concerns.

Collaborative problem-solving

I have adapted this principle from a remarkably helpful program for reducing parent-child conflict and solving family problems developed by Ross Greene and J. Stuart Ablon called Collaborative Problem Solving (CPS).[1] CPS begins with an acknowledgment of a child's concerns and her point of view. (A child's concern may be about feeling anxious or about something she felt was unfair.) This is followed by a statement of parents' concerns. (Parental concerns are often about health and safety, or about responsibilities.) Then, the child is invited to help solve the problem. Parents ask children for their ideas. "How do you think we can solve this problem?"

With this question, we have begun to change the channel in the child's mind. We have set in motion a movement *away* from a defensive or defiant attitude and *toward* a problem-solving attitude, and children now have an investment in the solution.

Collaborative problem-solving discussions are helpful to both parents and children. Parents develop a better understanding of the anxieties, frustrations, and disappointments that often lead to uncooperative or avoidant behavior. Children learn that rules are not arbitrary. They are reasonable and necessary for health, safety, and living together with greater harmony and less strife.

Greene and Ablon point out that parents and children rarely talk this way. Both children and parents do not directly state their concerns. Instead, they make "pronouncements." (For example, a child who does not want to go to school or a family outing will often say, "I'm not going." A parent is likely to respond, "Yes you are.")

Political opponents also rarely talk this way. Political opinions are pronouncements. In both family relationships and politics, pronouncements almost always lead to defensiveness and argument. Michael Mascolo's two professors debating gun control did not talk this way. Recall that, in ninety-one conversational turns, there were ninety pronouncements (statements of "adversarial positions") and *one* expression of a concern.[2]

Here is a shared concern in contemporary America. Both liberals and conservatives are concerned about the quality of American education, that American students are falling behind students from other countries on tests of reading, math, and general knowledge, and on graduation rates from high school and college, when we were once far ahead.

Liberals and conservatives, based on differences in temperament and worldview, have proposed different solutions to these problems. Liberal proposals are more "tender minded," focusing on providing greater academic and emotional support for low-performing students and schools, and finding creative ways to increase children's interest and engagement in learning. Conservative proposals are more "tough minded," focusing on accountability and setting higher standards, providing rewards for higher performance, and enforcing consequences for continued failure. Liberals are likely to believe that failing students and failing schools do not receive enough public support. Conservatives are more likely to believe that students are insufficiently challenged, promoted without having achieved a minimum standard of competence, and are not required to work hard.

This is now a pragmatic discussion, a discussion of how to achieve a mutually agreed upon goal. In a discussion of concerns, the complexity of a problem can be recognized; facts can be presented and conclusions can be debated; programs to achieve improved performance in different parts of the country and the world can be studied and their relevance and generalizability can be tested; shared principles of successful programs and the mistakes of unsuccessful programs can be identified. In our best discussions, we will acknowledge the limits of what we know and accept the possibility that we might be wrong.

In a discussion of concerns, it is likely that we will find truth on both sides and from multiple perspectives; we may arrive at unexpected insights, not predicted by either approach. And, with appropriate humility, we will agree on the need to know more. In this case, recent evidence suggests that both sides are right. Children need *both* higher standards *and* more support; students need greater engagement in learning, and schools need greater accountability. Successful schools, both public and private, provide both high levels of support and high standards for success.

Even our most vehement culture war debates have a different quality when stated as concerns. Many conservatives, for example, are deeply concerned about the decline in patriotic feeling in America. Conservative politicians express outrage when children in public schools are taught what is wrong with American society, past and present. Stated as an opinion, we are likely to have an angry, contemptuous, and unproductive exchange. Stated as a concern ("I want my children to be proud of their country" or "I'm concerned that when we teach critical race theory, my children will no longer feel pride in being an American") a different kind of discussion is possible.

A liberal can then express her concern on this issue. ("If children don't know the full extent of racial discrimination or our cruel treatment of Native Americans, they will not have an accurate understanding of American history, and they will lack understanding and compassion for victims of injustice.) Stated as a concern, this issue is still difficult to talk about and may evoke vehement disagreement. But the concern is understandable, and discussion is therefore possible.

Intellectual charity

10

What are your opponents' most reasonable arguments?

The principle of intellectual charity is fundamental to reasoned argument. Intellectual charity is not about being compassionate or kind. This principle states that, in any discussion, we should acknowledge and accept the best version of an opponent's ideas, not an exaggerated or distorted version, a "straw man."[1]

In *The Coddling of the American Mind*, Greg Lukianoff and Jonathan Haidt emphasize this principle in their recommendations for nurturing "wiser kids," "wiser universities," and "wiser societies." Lukianoff and Haidt argue, with good evidence, that a generation of students has been raised to believe that their feelings are always right, that disagreement is unsafe, that the world is divided between good people and bad people, a righteous "us" and an evil "them," and to take the most offensive instead of the most charitable interpretation of personal slights and differences of opinion.

Intellectual charity is an antidote to what Lukianoff and Haidt call the "great untruth" of emotional reasoning. Emotional reasoning equates the effect of a statement (I feel offended) with the intent of the speaker. They correctly warn that this cognitive distortion has harmful consequences – for learning from others, for personal relationships, and for our emotional health.[2]

Uncharitable argument, however, is far more widespread than on college campuses. Adherence to the principle of charity is rare in contemporary American politics. Exaggeration and distortion

DOI: 10.4324/9781032679075-13

of opposing opinions, always present to some degree in political debates, have become the standard form of political argument. Our political divide is fueled by caricatures, consciously or unconsciously drawn, of what others actually believe and why they believe what they do.

Once we have committed ourselves to understanding someone else's opinions in their most reasonable form, we are engaged in a different kind of listening. We now enter a conversation with an attitude of "what can I learn from this person who I may disagree with?" and "is there something right about what they are saying, even if I believe that their opinions are mostly wrong?"

Philosopher Gary Gutting points out that intellectual charity, because it engages someone's most reasonable ideas, allows us to make more persuasive arguments, beyond simple assertions of our opinion. (An argument, Gutting reminds us, "is not a bludgeon to beat opponents into submission, but a tool for intellectual development."[3] Or, as Tina Fey says in *Mean Girls*, "calling someone stupid doesn't make you any smarter."[4]) Gutting may be overly optimistic about this advantage of intellectual charity. Uncharitable arguments are often emotionally compelling and therefore succeed in their purpose. But, in some cases, he may be right.

The principle of charity (and the companion principle of intellectual humility) requires moral and intellectual effort. This principle of reasoned argument is always difficult for politicians, especially when running for office, who want to show that their opponents are unreasonable or that their ideas are dangerous. To get elected, you may not want to acknowledge that your opponent is reasonable, even when she is. Extremists and demagogues knowingly abandon the principle of charity.

A common form of non-charitable argument is to exaggerate your opponent's views, then ridicule this caricature. Sarah Palin's claim that Barack Obama's health-care proposals would establish "death panels" is a well-known example of partisan caricature. Ted Kennedy's description of Robert Bork's opinions during Bork's Supreme Court confirmation hearing in 1987 is a frequently cited example of liberal distortion, justifiably infamous among conservatives.[5]

There are other, less obvious, forms of uncharitable thought and debate. In making an argument, we may choose an extreme opinion and then claim (or imply) that this idea represents all liberals or all conservatives. The more partisan we become, the more often we will engage in this form of uncharitable argument. We will be looking for extreme examples of opposing ideas.

This strategy is sometimes cynical; the person speaking or writing knows what they are doing. When challenged, they have a ready defense; they are not lying, because *someone did* say this. (Arguments of this kind are especially prevalent on partisan news media and social media posts.) In other cases, we may sincerely believe that the extremists *are* representative of the opposing group. Because it is often difficult to know how widespread a particular idea or attitude is among members of any group, this form of uncharitable argument can also be very persuasive (especially, when people are afraid).

Uncharitable interpretation is a danger whenever we characterize liberals or conservatives as a group. We find examples of this fallacy almost daily, not only in partisan politics and on social media, but in books and punditry by thoughtful people who (should) know better.

False dichotomies and "angry science"

Another common form of uncharitable argument is one-sided presentation of facts. We present only facts that support our side and, intentionally or through ignorance, omit other facts. This form of argument can also be persuasive. How many of us know all the facts relevant to any issue or problem?

A more subtle form of uncharitable argument is to create a false dichotomy. In all the fields of which I have more than a rudimentary understanding – psychology, parenting, education, and politics – false dichotomies are common. We seem to need to think this way.

Dichotomies have some usefulness. In their helpful forms, dichotomies provide initial clarity and a beginning framework for understanding different approaches to problems. Political dichotomies and labels (for example, the dichotomy of liberal and conservative political attitudes) allow us to identify ourselves and describe a general bias in how we think about the world. In life, dichotomies are often necessary. We need to choose sides; there are votes to be cast and political battles that need to be fought. At the same time, however, dichotomies are often false. Real-world problems are rarely either/or.

Daniel Kahneman described a common form of uncharitable scientific debate he called, "angry science." In angry science, scientists publish the results of their experiments and conclusions based on their research. Opponents then challenge the conclusions. In Kahneman's experience, scientific opponents often present "a summary caricature of the target position, refute the weakest argument in that caricature and declare the total destruction of the adversary's position." The argument then continues in repeated exchanges, no resolution is achieved, and no one changes their mind.[6]

I have not found a better description of our political arguments.

This kind of debate is an accepted model of scientific progress. When it is successful, new facts emerge and theories are revised, leading to better theories and new facts. Kahneman believes, however, that this is usually not what happens. More often, this process results only in making people angry and losing friends.

Scientific debates remain unresolved for understandable reasons. There is almost always some uncertainty in the interpretation of any experiment. Scientific results, especially in social science, are always conditional, subject to limitations of methodology or the generalizability of data. A scientist can continue to believe that, even if results contrary to her hypothesis are true in one case, they may be disproved by subsequent research. Her core conviction therefore remains unchallenged. This is why "people never change their mind."[7]

Kahneman recommends an alternative method he calls, "adversarial collaboration." In an adversarial collaboration, scientists holding different beliefs agree to jointly design experiments that will resolve their disagreement. Adversarial collaboration is not a simple compromise between opposing opinions. It is an effort to resolve a disagreement with new evidence, for example, to specify the conditions under which the results are observed. When we engage in this form of collaboration, we are likely to find that the answer to the disagreement is "sometimes yes, sometimes no." Kahneman argues that this is a much better route toward scientific progress.

Almost all successful discussions of difficult topics and resolution of disagreements – between spouses, between parents and children, and between political opponents – begin with (or move toward) a charitable understanding of another person's point of view, an effort to appreciate the concerns that animate their opinions, and to move beyond false dichotomies. There are reasonable arguments on both sides of many divisive issues in American politics – on taxes and business regulations, on raising the minimum wage, on immigration, on affirmative action, on abortion, and on almost all questions of foreign policy.

As with all the recommendations for reasoned argument I will offer, there are limits to this principle. Not every charitable understanding is correct. We still have the right to strong opinions and deep disagreements about what is right and wrong. We have the right to pass judgment on someone's behavior, to call out dishonesty and hypocrisy, and to identify offensive and dangerous ideas. We have the right to be angry at injustice.

But we should at least consider a charitable understanding. Even when we conclude that our opponent is hypocritical, that her arguments are rationalizations of self-interest (or the interests of lobbyists and donors) or an excuse for bigotry, we should first consider that, perhaps, they are not.

Intellectual humility   **11**

What are the limits of your beliefs?

As a companion to the principle of charity, we also need to cultivate an attitude of intellectual humility. I am using the word humility both in its common meaning and in a more specific sense. We should begin with personal humility – recognizing the limits of our ability or virtue, that others know more than we do, and that, in any specific instance, we might be wrong. Humility in this sense ("I don't know enough about this problem" or "I could be wrong") is an essential element of constructive discussion, an antidote to pathological certainty, and almost entirely absent from current political arguments, at all levels.[1]

What are the limits of your political philosophy?

I would like to add an additional meaning of intellectual humility that is especially relevant to political debates. We should regard it as axiomatic that every ideology and every political belief has limits. Intellectual humility requires that we make a sustained effort to specify the limits of our opinions and beliefs. Intellectual humility asks, "What are the limits of my beliefs?"

An attitude of humility requires that we recognize the complexity of most social and political problems. Intellectual humility is based on the understanding that every policy, domestic or international,

DOI: 10.4324/9781032679075-14

is likely to have both good and bad effects. Every policy will help some people and impose costs on others. Every policy will address some priorities but not others. Every policy or course of action is likely to have unanticipated and unintended consequences. In the real world, "visions" and philosophies break down; there are almost always exceptions and valid competing concerns. Humility requires an awareness that there are other perspectives we may not have considered.

Humility builds guardrails against extremism and contempt. Intellectual humility makes us "moderate" in the best sense of the word, even when we believe that some problems require bold actions. Intellectual humility allows us to defy the gravitational pull of tribalism and to see each problem with its unique pros and cons.

If we are liberal, we need to ask, what are the limits of my liberalism? Where in my liberalism can I find a place for conservative priorities and concerns? How can my empathy and compassion be reconciled with the need for safety and security, for the maintenance of traditions and established norms? When do I need to be more tough minded? When have liberal attitudes and policies failed or gone too far?

If we are conservative, we need to ask, what are the limits of my conservatism? Where in my conservatism can I find a place for liberal priorities and concerns? What am I willing to do, *now*, to alleviate suffering and injustice, to foster greater tolerance of different identities and lifestyles?

Both liberals and conservatives need to ask, have I considered the possible unintended consequences of my proposals and recommendations? Have I considered all other perspectives? Most social problems have multiple causes and uncertain solutions. Often, especially when we are influenced by fear or resentment, or a feeling of injustice, we find a single cause that *feels* right to us, a cause or a solution to a problem that supports our biases, and we ignore other possible causes.

Many conservative writers regard humility as a foundational principle of political conservatism and a reason for their belief in limited government. These writers argue that the wisdom of existing institutions and traditions is superior to progressive plans, based on abstract principles, to create a better society. This is a different meaning of humility. It is important for liberals to be humble about the wisdom of their proposals for political and social change, but the humility these writers recommend can be (and has been) misused as a rationalization for the protection of privilege and an unjust status quo. When we adhere to the principle of intellectual humility, we will also be humble about the wisdom of existing institutions and traditional social norms. It goes without saying that a free-market economy has brought freedom and prosperity to many but has also tolerated injustices and left many human problems unsolved. In the sense that I am speaking of humility, an unquestioned belief in the wisdom of traditions *that does not specify the limits and conditions of this belief* is not humility, but a form of certainty.

Intellectual humility does not ask us to change our beliefs, only to recognize their limits. Conservatives believe, as a core principle, in limited government. There are many ways, however, to define "limited." Even the most ardent conservative or libertarian is likely to admit that some regulations are required to protect public health and safety. Most people accept the need for regulations to prevent the disposal of toxic waste near school playgrounds and the use of carcinogenic and neurotoxic chemicals in foods and household products. Conservatives are less likely to support many of these regulations, citing current or long-term economic costs; but this is now a pragmatic, not an ideological, debate.

Even the most committed liberal is likely to accept that compassion also has limits. Some limits on social welfare spending are necessary, and limits on immigration and political asylum are also necessary, in some circumstances. These policies, motivated by compassion and fundamental to a liberal worldview, may have costs or consequences that undermine other compassionate priorities.

If you are conservative and believe in limited government as a guiding principle, intellectual humility requires that you identify when, and in what forms, active government intervention is legitimate and necessary. If you are liberal and believe in affirmative action to promote diversity in education and employment, intellectual humility requires that you consider the limits of affirmative action. Under what conditions is affirmative action inappropriate, unhelpful, or counterproductive? In our current political debates, these obvious exceptions and limitations to our priorities and worldview are rarely publicly acknowledged.

Intellectual humility – an awareness and careful consideration of alternative perspectives – is an important aspect of what it means to be educated or an expert in any field. An educated person is able to understand more aspects of any complex problem. The temptation to simplify is always present, and simplification is sometimes helpful and necessary. But most problems are complex; both causes and solutions are often uncertain. Ideologues and partisans consider only one possible cause and only one possible outcome when assessing problems or making judgments. Experts recognize that the causes of social problems are complex and often cyclical; each cause has multiple effects, which then act as new causes. Experts, of course, can be wrong, for many reasons, subject to bias and even financial pressure. *But the thought processes of an expert and an ideologue are essentially different.*

We could all use more intellectual charity and intellectual humility. Our society needs self-questioning liberals and self-questioning conservatives. In our current moment, we have too few of each. Our political culture is dominated instead, on both sides, by self-righteousness and pathological certainty.

If you are a liberal student who believes that conservative speakers should not be invited to your college because their ideas or words may be hurtful, you need to ask yourself, what are the limits of this belief? And who has the right to decide, in any given instance, what ideas are dangerous, and how should a tolerant society address this difficult question? And when are threats or assaults on speakers justified in the name of opposition to ideas that you believe are harmful or support oppression? (The answer is never.) If you are not willing to think about these questions, and if you are not being challenged to consider that there may be other perspectives on issues in addition to your own, then you are not educated, even if you are a student at Berkeley, Harvard, Brown, or Yale.

If you are conservative and learn of abusive messages and threats sent to people who oppose your views, and you are unwilling to publicly condemn this vicious and dangerous behavior, this is equally disgraceful, and you are also not educated.

The principle of humility may be the most challenging of all the principles of constructive argument. Although experts in many fields routinely think this way, for example, in economics and medicine (and, sometimes, psychology), political activists and the general public most often do not. It is easier to argue than to listen, to surround ourselves with only like-minded people, to read or listen only to those who confirm what we already believe and tell us what we want to hear, to believe what we want to believe "and disregard the rest."[2] It is easier to simply choose sides, to give our side the benefit of the doubt, and regard the other side with contempt.

Perspectivism

A philosophical statement of the principle of intellectual humility can be found in the writings of Friedrich Nietzsche and William James. Nietzsche, referring more generally to a theory of truth, called this idea, "perspectivism."[3] He argued that there is no unbiased perception of the world. We are always seeing and understanding events from a particular point of view – a perspective that reveals some aspects of reality and obscures others, that each perspective is based on a *feeling*, and that the more perspectives we have about the world, the more objective our perception will be. William James expressed a similar idea, that "each observer gains a partial superiority of insight from the particular position in which he stands."[4]

My colleague Arnold Zinman offered this analogy: If we are looking at a sculpture from any single vantage point, we get a partial view. We see part of the sculpture in more detail and notice nuances in its form and expression. But it is still only one perspective. To view the whole sculpture and understand the relationship of its parts, we need to walk around it.

If we take the principle of perspectivism seriously, we will be able to listen with greater openness to the opinions of others. We will understand more, and we will be more modest and temperate about our own ideas.

On liberal college campuses and on social media, it has become common for students to be told, "check your privilege." This usually means that we should be aware of how our attitudes have been influenced by social advantages that others do not have. If said in a non-judgmental spirit, to encourage humility and self-examination, this admonition may be warranted and helpful.

I would add, however, when we are expressing political opinions, a more important recommendation: "check your certainty." Be aware of the extent to which you may have failed to consider other perspectives and the limits of your beliefs. Especially, "check your contempt."

From ideology to pragmatism

12

A better grammar for political debates

If we are willing, first, to listen to another person's concerns, then, to consider the most reasonable form of her opinion (intellectual charity) and to acknowledge the inevitable limitations of our own (intellectual humility), we have taken several steps away from ideology toward pragmatism. Our discussion will now more often be "pragmatic."

I am using the word pragmatism in a specific sense. I am not speaking about being pragmatic as a political tactic – deciding what issues should be given priority and what battles to choose, or a willingness to compromise, or having modest goals, or a recognition that there are limits to what can be accomplished at any time. Being pragmatic in these ways is often necessary. But I am writing now about pragmatism in a meaning closer to its philosophical origin in the writings of William James – that truth is not found in abstract principles or beliefs, but in effects that can be observed. Pragmatism is about what works and what doesn't.

Pragmatism is anti-ideological and an alternative to certainty. The language of pragmatism is conditional, not absolute. Pragmatism asks about specific conditions. To change an ideological statement – a statement of conviction or belief – into a pragmatic question, we ask, "in what cases, under what conditions, to what extent."

DOI: 10.4324/9781032679075-15

Pragmatic debates are very different from ideological debates. Ideology imposes constraints on thought and problem-solving. Ideology limits the problems we see, the stories we listen to, and the solutions we are willing to consider. Pragmatism removes these constraints. Pragmatism continues asking questions. Pragmatism, James wrote, is open-minded.

Pragmatism is a way of thinking that attempts to understand problems with as little bias and as few preconceptions as possible. Pragmatism recognizes that most problems have multiple causes and that most proposed solutions have multiple effects. Ideology offers quick and simple answers to complex problems. Pragmatism requires research and study, a commitment to consider *all* the facts, a willingness to admit mistakes, and to change our minds. Ideology is easy; pragmatism is hard.

Pragmatic questions are "how" questions. "How" questions attempt to identify pathways (and impediments) to solutions. "How" questions are empirical, scientific questions: "What will happen if, under these circumstances, we do this?" "What will be the short-term and long-term effects of this policy?" "Have we considered all the relevant facts and possible consequences of this course of action?"[1] Pragmatism evaluates pros and cons.

When we acknowledge the limits of our ideology, it is no longer ideology. We will still have guiding principles, sympathies, priorities, and concerns. But priorities are not the same as ideologies. They may be passionate and urgent priorities, but, unlike ideologies, priorities are not absolute. Pragmatism prefers a grammar of "both/and" instead of "either/or." We are not asking whether or not, but when, how, or how much.

Pragmatism is also intrinsically nonpartisan. The solution to one problem may be a conservative solution; the solution to another problem may be a liberal solution. If it works, it doesn't matter whether the idea came from the right or the left. In debating legislation, politicians may, at times, engage in pragmatic discussions, to some degree. But these discussions are rarely fully pragmatic. They are still constrained by partisanship and ideology. If the solution to any problem is predetermined to be a conservative or liberal solution, thought has been constrained. Too often, for many of us, finding the cause of a problem means finding someone to blame. Finding a single cause or assigning blame is almost always based on ideology, not pragmatism.

Pragmatism also reduces our tendency toward ad hominem attacks. Our disagreement is about how to solve a problem, not who you are. The farther toward either end of the ideological spectrum we move, the farther we have moved away from pragmatism.

I am not advocating humility and pragmatism as substitutes for ambitious policies and inspiring ideals. We need political leaders, both conservative and liberal, who are able to articulate a vision of a better society that helps bring us closer together. The struggles of American families and children I will discuss in the final chapter of this book will require ambitious, pragmatic solutions.

Pragmatism and science

Pragmatism is scientific, in the best sense of the word. Science accepts that our knowledge is incomplete, and we do not have all the answers. (Ideologues believe that they do.) Science considers alternative hypotheses and different ways of solving problems. *Cherry-picking facts to support a desired, a priori conclusion is pseudoscientific and not pragmatism.* In a recent lecture, Supreme Court Justice Amy Coney Barrett identified a similar tendency in constitutional law. Barrett warned that the use of history in making legal decisions risks "looking out over a crowd and picking out our friends."[2]

Cherry-picking of facts by partisans is often a conscious strategy, a sophisticated form of lying. Cherry-picking may be unavoidable for most of us, much of the time. It is difficult for any of us to know all the facts necessary to understand or solve a problem, and confirmation bias will always be present, to some degree.

We can never be entirely pragmatic. Our temperament or our vision of human nature will still be present in our thinking. Our values and worldview select the questions we ask and the solutions we prefer. Even when we accept the principle of pragmatism, we will still *feel* differently about important problems and proposed solutions, and we will still disagree. The only answer to this universal tendency in human thought is to cultivate greater humility – to be aware of the limits of our knowledge – that there may be facts we do not know and aspects of a problem we are not aware of.

Social science is less certain in its conclusions than physical sciences, for many reasons. The findings of social science have been observed in less controlled settings and may reflect particular social conditions. It is more difficult to establish whether the same observations will be true when conditions change and whether all the relevant factors have been considered. In social science research, it is easier to find correlations than causes. It is difficult to study the multiple effects of proposed interventions; policies designed to solve one problem may impede the solution of others.

Still, social science is both possible and necessary. Dedicated, impartial scientists and policy analysts do this work every day, in psychology, economics, education, public health, and other fields. These scientists may, in some instances, be incorrect in their assessments and recommendations. At times, there are scandals (for example, inappropriate approval of drugs and toxic chemicals) leading to catastrophic consequences for citizens. But to demean or mistrust scientists and their work is wrong. It is disheartening that this sentence even needs to be written.[3]

Of course, not all the problems that divide us are pragmatic or scientific questions. We are also divided by moral and cultural issues, and science cannot solve moral problems. Abortion and marriage equality are moral or religious questions, not scientific problems. Economic disagreements are also not entirely pragmatic. To conservatives, proposals to raise taxes on the very wealthy *feel* anti-capitalist, punishing successful businesses and entrepreneurs who, from a conservative perspective, have created our prosperity and deserve our thanks. It does not *feel* this way to liberals. To liberals, our current economic inequality feels fundamentally wrong.

Government welfare programs, beyond a certain minimum, do not feel right to many American conservatives. To most liberals, government programs that attempt to reduce current poverty, improve the life chances of children born into poverty, and offer universal health insurance are moral imperatives.

Despite these philosophical differences, economic problems are, in principle or in part, pragmatic problems. How to promote sustained economic growth – more jobs that provide a path toward a secure and hopeful future for more people – is a pragmatic question that can be studied, and the effectiveness of different policies can, at least partially, be decided by evidence.

Conservatives, historically and continuing into the present, generally propose lower taxes and less regulation of businesses, both on ideological and on pragmatic grounds. The ideological argument was succinctly stated by George W. Bush. ("It's not the government's money, it's your money.") The pragmatic argument is that tax cuts encourage business investment and consumer spending, with benefits that spread throughout the economy, and that excessive regulations slow the creation and expansion of businesses that provide jobs.

Liberals, ideologically, believe in the responsibility of government to help improve the lives of less advantaged citizens in the here and now. The pragmatic argument is that government interventions in the economy – investments in education, science, and infrastructure that private companies are unable or have less incentive to do; ending discrimination; ensuring safe and humane working conditions and a higher minimum wage; financial support to people who are poor; and regulations to protect public health – are necessary, both in the short-term and long-term, to stimulate widely shared opportunity and economic growth.[4]

There is a lot of room for disagreement in these ideas. We will disagree about what constitutes humane and unjust. We will disagree about whether (and to what extent) reducing inequality is a desirable goal. We will disagree about what aspects of economic and social life should be (and to what extent) supported or regulated by the government or by the private sector.

These are important and passionate disagreements, with profound consequences for our daily lives. These are the arguments we used to have, in less polarized times. We are arguing about the sources of our prosperity and freedom, and how to preserve and extend them. But these questions are, again, in principle, pragmatic. These are the arguments that our best opinion and political leaders are attempting to restore.

Make a small change

There are additional steps we can take to help us move away from ideology toward pragmatism. We can begin with a small change.

In my work with families, I often ask spouses, parents, children, and teenagers to make a small change in their behavior in response to another person's concerns or point of view. In family relationships, a small change can have large effects. The changes I encourage are more than "transactional" compromises. Transactional compromises ("If you do this for me, I'll do this for you") can be helpful in resolving some family disagreements. A child, for example, might agree not to use hurtful language or to accept additional responsibility with family chores; in return, parents allow him to stay up later or spend additional time watching television or playing video games. This is also a common form of political compromise – each side gives the other some of what they want.

These simple compromises are sometimes helpful in a more important way. With a successful compromise, we have established for children the *principle of compromise* as an alternative to coercive tactics. Children learn an important life lesson – that compromise is necessary for family harmony and, more generally, for getting along with others.

Transactional compromises, however, are often transient and superficial, and leave underlying feelings of resentment and unfairness unresolved. What we are working toward is a different kind of change – a change in a child or parent's behavior that *acknowledges the legitimacy of another person's needs, feelings, or concerns.*

This is often not as difficult as it seems. Most teens, for example, even when they are angry and defiant, acknowledge that some family rules – and punishments for violations of rules – are necessary and appropriate in some instances. (Almost all children accept that punishments are sometimes justified. They just believe that their brother or sister is the one who should be punished.) Most parents are willing to grant their children and teens greater autonomy, in some circumstances.

When family members or political opponents are unwilling to make a small change, feelings of unfairness and blaming of others have become deeply ingrained, and the legitimacy of an opponent's concerns (or, in families, respect for parental authority) has eroded. A small change helps arrest this malignant process.

Like a gesture of empathy, a small change has the potential to set in motion a virtuous cycle in family relationships. Families are now, at least for that moment, unstuck from argument and mutual grievance. Increased cooperation from children elicits more frequent expressions of appreciation from parents. Feelings of anger and resentment are more easily repaired, leading to greater hopefulness, sharing of interests, and expressions of pride. In this way, we have created a therapeutic "butterfly effect" in family relationships.

Defy gravity

In politics, a strong feeling or opinion on a single issue exerts a gravitational pull on other issues, perhaps more strongly now than in previous decades.[5] The gravitational pull of ideology and partisanship has both emotional and intellectual causes. Partisanship offers feelings of acceptance and belonging, deep intrinsic needs and a powerful force in human psychology. Political partisanship also has some practical usefulness. Party loyalty may be necessary for getting things done (but may quickly become malignant when we feel threatened or disrespected).

There are also intellectual reasons for gravitational pull. Once we have identified a basic principle or concern, we will tend to apply this principle to other issues and problems. When we become aware of an injustice, we now see other issues in the light of injustice. When we feel that our way of life is threatened, we will be more aware of other instances where the need to defend ourselves is a priority. Disillusionment is also likely to spread. When we become disillusioned with one liberal or conservative cause, cynicism is likely to color our attitudes toward other issues and causes. (This is very common in adolescents who have become disillusioned in adults they once admired.)

David French has described a form of political bias he calls, "the normal partisan mind."[6] It works this way: Once we have identified with a political party, any bad actions by members of our party (for example, behavior that is dishonest, unethical, extremist, or racist) are regarded as an exception. We believe (or pretend to believe) that these actions do not represent who we really are or what we really stand for. The same statements and actions by our opponents, however, are regarded as emblematic, revealing their true nature. This bias is an intellectual expression of tribalism and a subtle, but very common, form of hypocrisy.

It is possible, however, to defy the gravitational pull of partisanship. I have argued that there are common themes – organizing feelings and principles – that explain much of the consistency of our political opinions. For most of us, however, these principles have limits and exceptions. Pragmatism requires that we consider each issue on its own terms, with its own unique set of facts and reasons.

Listening and compromise also have a gravitational pull but, unfortunately, a far weaker one. The experience of finding a collaborative solution offers an emotional satisfaction that serves as a countervailing force to tribalism. After negotiating a limited bipartisan bill for the reduction of gun violence, Democratic Senator Kyrsten Sinema said to her Republican colleague John Cornyn, "What's next, John."

Take the hypocrisy test

Hypocrisy is rampant in politics, even more than we recognize. Political hypocrisy is the pursuit of partisan advantage disguised as principle. We are hypocritical because we don't want to admit this.

The hypocrisy test is intellectually simple but emotionally difficult. We will often fail this test. We need to ask ourselves: How would I feel if someone I support acted in this way?

Hypocrisy is an extreme version of the normal partisan mind. We are all susceptible to hypocrisy. The more partisan we become, the more likely we will become hypocritical. When we need our side to win at almost any cost, we will find reasons to overlook or excuse egregious conduct by those we support, conduct we would condemn in an opponent, and we will more easily perceive the hypocrisy of our opponents.

The hypocrisy of politicians is often conscious and calculated. Many conservatives in the 1990s said that they could not vote for Bill Clinton because "character matters"; then, in 2016, they supported Donald Trump. In March 2016, Mitch McConnell refused to take up Barack Obama's nomination of Merrick Garland to the Supreme Court, based on the principle that a Supreme Court nomination should not be considered by the Senate in the final months of an election year. Four years later, the Senate, under McConnell's leadership, confirmed Donald Trump's nomination of Amy Coney Barrett in September. McConnell's "principle" was simply made up for the moment, then dropped when inconvenient. These well-known examples are flagrant fouls – blatant examples of partisan hypocrisy.

Here is an example of liberal hypocrisy: Over the past several decades, many universities have established speech codes to protect students from offensive language and verbal harassment. But they have often not protected conservative students. David French reports that, as a student at Harvard Law School, he was "booed, hissed, and told to 'go die'" for expressing pro-life opinions. French tells us that "exactly zero administrators cared about my feelings."[7]

Often, however, we are not aware of our hypocrisy. We may sincerely believe that we are impartial or convince ourselves that we are guided by principle, not self-interest, or that this instance is different.

Hypocrisy can be avoided only when there is a genuine commitment to a higher principle, when there is "we" that transcends, or at least competes with, an "I." Hypocrisy may be especially prevalent now, as values that transcend partisanship (for example, belief in the democratic process) have eroded, and we regard our opponents as an existential threat. The best solution to the problem of hypocrisy is, again, intellectual humility – to be aware of our tendency toward hypocrisy, which is present whenever we feel strongly that something is right or wrong, and to have the honesty (and for partisans, the courage) to call out corruption and extremism on our own side.

Educational success in Mississippi: A triumph of pragmatism

Nicholas Kristof reports an instructive example of the benefits of prag-matism. Mississippi is one of the poorest states in the country. Despite this poverty, since the early 2000s, the state has achieved remarkable progress in teaching children to read. Kristof reports, "Mississippi fourth graders now are tied for best performers in the nation [on] national tests of reading and rank second in math." Mississippi has also significantly increased high school graduation rates.

The reading intervention that produced these gains has many components: Mississippi uses a curriculum that emphasizes phonics and the science of reading, a method supported by decades of research (but opposed, until very recently, by some influential reading specialists). The intervention is supported by the state's teachers and teachers' union and includes administrative oversight to make sure that the program is being implemented correctly. Increased professional development for teachers is also part of the program. Pre-K programs for kids in low-income areas were started, with pre-K teachers paid at the same rate as elementary school teachers. Each child's progress is closely monitored, and those who are not making progress receive additional tutoring.

A central aspect of the program is a state-wide third-grade reading exam that all students must pass before moving on to fourth grade. This exam was initially controversial, but proved highly successful – kids, teachers, and parents were galvanized to put in more effort, with enthusiasm like that of playing in a championship football game. Students who don't pass the exam are able to take it a second time; if they fail again, they can attend summer school and take it a third time. By the end of the summer, 91% of students pass. Those who don't pass and repeat third grade show significant progress a few years later. Other components of the intervention were not effective and therefore dropped from the program.[8]

The success of this program is not based on a philosophy of edu-cation, but on demonstrated effectiveness, evaluated at every stage. Science and pragmatism have triumphed over ideology, improving the lives of thousands of children.

Finding common ground

Part IV

In politics, again, it is almost a commonplace, that a party of order or stability, and a party of progress or reform, are both necessary elements of a healthy state of political life.... Each of these modes of thinking derives its utility from the deficiencies of the other; but it is in a great measure the opposition of the other that keeps each within the limits of reason and sanity.

John Stuart Mill, *On Liberty*

DOI: 10.4324/9781032679075-16

Liberalism and conservatism in modern American politics
13

Pragmatic liberalism and compassionate conservatism

Disagreement over the role of government in a democratic society has been a defining difference between conservatives and liberals for most of the 20th century. This is how the debate between liberal and conservative political parties has most often been framed – as a difference between liberal ("big government") and conservative ("small government") political philosophies. I have argued that this debate, although important, is not the underlying deep grammar of our political differences. Arguments about the size of the government have emotional roots. Often, these are attitudes toward social and economic inequality and poverty.

The central problems for the conservative sensibility – the "party of order and stability" – from the Optimates of Rome to contemporary conservatives – are the problems of poverty and injustice. If the conservative sensibility, as many argue, is based on "wise stewardship" of our cultural and institutional heritage,[1] the question is, when confronted with poverty and injustice, what should we do? Historically, conservatism has largely avoided this problem. There is considerable evidence that acceptance of inequality, in all forms, is a core dimension of conservative politics, in all

DOI: 10.4324/9781032679075-17

countries. Arthur C. Brooks notes that most conservatives accept this stereotype.

But this is not true of all conservatives. Several contemporary conservatives have argued that the common view of conservatism is false. These writers believe that conservatism is (or can be) equally compassionate – and, in some respects, more genuinely compassionate – than liberalism. These writers have presented, in different forms, a philosophy of compassionate conservatism that may help us find common ground.

Heroic conservatism

Michael Gerson has presented a case for compassionate conservatism, he calls, "heroic conservatism."[2] Gerson was a speechwriter for George W. Bush and a passionate advocate in the Bush administration for the policies of compassionate conservatism. For Gerson, conservatism is a heroic project, based on idealism, universal human dignity, and religious faith. He argues for policies that combine traditional conservative values and humanitarian ideals – programs that include active government efforts to reduce global poverty and illness, and to defend freedom internationally – among its core priorities and goals. Compassion – a resolve to improve the lives of people who are left out of American prosperity – is a central tenet of Gerson's policy agenda.

The most significant achievement of Gerson's compassionate conservatism was the development of an ambitious program to save lives through the prevention and treatment of AIDS in Africa (PEPFAR), now acknowledged by liberals as perhaps the most successful humanitarian program in history.[3] Gerson cites other achievements based on the philosophy of compassionate conservatism – efforts to improve educational success for American children with higher standards and increased accountability (No Child Left Behind); faith-based initiatives to help religious institutions provide mentoring, after-school programs, and social services in poor communities; and the addition of prescription drug coverage in Medicare. Gerson regards his policies as conservative because of their basis in religious faith, his commitment to the principle of limited government, and his belief that many liberals had abandoned religion as a source of political inspiration and ideals. He explains,

> I am conservative because I believe in the accumulated wisdom of humanity… when ideals and institutions are casually discarded in the cause of personal liberation, the result is usually personal suffering and social decay.[4]

Gerson reports that this humanitarian vision of conservatism was opposed, even regarded with disdain, by many traditional conservatives, especially Republican congressional leaders. He contrasts a conservative philosophy of limited government with a dogmatic anti-government ideology. He presents compassionate conservatism as a middle ground between secular liberalism and a "libertarian ideology of indifference."

Liberals will certainly disagree with many of Gerson's ideas. A liberal is likely to question the scope and effectiveness of Gerson's domestic proposals. Are they adequate to meet our needs? A liberal will ask, for example, why Gerson's compassionate conservatism enacted prescription drug coverage for Medicare but did not propose some form of universal health insurance. Most liberals will strongly disagree with Gerson's pro-life beliefs.

There are false dichotomies and uncharitable arguments in Gerson's description of the opinions of his opponents (and unwarranted certainty in his own). Gerson writes, for example, that liberal support for abortion rights "has more to do with power and autonomy than compassion"; that many secular liberals believe there are "no truths we can know with certainty"; that the central political argument of our time is between idealism and cynicism; and that it takes a "long and difficult search" to find the moral idealism of Hubert Humphrey in today's Democratic party. Liberals will reply that these are caricatures of their motives and beliefs, and that although modern liberalism is predominantly secular, moral idealism remains central to a liberal worldview, as it has been throughout the history of liberal thought.

Still, these are disagreements we can talk about, based on shared values and concerns. Gerson's heroic conservatism is ambitious and idealistic. Liberals will find common ground in his commitment to ending poverty and improving education for American children. Sadly, Michael Gerson died recently at a young age, and America lost a passionate and caring voice in our national conversation.

The conservative heart

Arthur C. Brooks, former president of the American Enterprise Institute, has presented a case for compassionate conservatism he calls, *The Conservative Heart*. Brooks tells a story of American history – a story of unparalleled growth and prosperity, of excessive regulations that now stifle entrepreneurship, and of welfare programs that are counterproductive, creating a culture of dependency on government support. For Brooks, we have a choice – between the dynamism, wealth, and freedom of free enterprise and the stagnation of profligate government spending. This is the paradigmatic conservative narrative of prosperity in America.

Brooks challenges both liberals and traditional conservatives. He believes that liberal policies to reduce poverty are misguided and have therefore failed. Conservatives, however, have not presented either a moral language of compassion or a practical agenda to help the poor.[5]

Brooks argues for a "steely-edged" compassion – a compassion that offers help to the truly needy (the words needy or indigent in Brooks' book are almost always qualified by the adjective "truly") but also demands work and personal responsibility, because these values offer the best hope for escaping poverty. These arguments for conservative policies are, at first glance, entirely pragmatic. Brooks believes that conservative policies work and liberal policies don't, and a conservative compassion more effectively achieves a shared humanitarian goal – that everyone can become more prosperous, "especially those who need relief the most."

Brooks' arguments illustrate both opportunities and obstacles to a more constructive discussion and finding common ground.

Brooks' steely edge will feel too sharp to most liberals. A pragmatic liberalism, however, must listen to Brooks' story and address his concerns.

The most significant problems with Brooks' vision are his reliance on false dichotomies and his selective presentation of evidence to support his views. Brooks writes, for example, that liberal efforts to alleviate poverty are based on a "materialistic, mechanistic" view of human nature. He argues that liberals view the poor as "a burden to be managed" and think of poverty as a "quantifiable concept." In contrast, a conservative philosophy "takes a uniquely holistic view of human dignity." He tells us that there are "two kinds of people... those who believe in work as punishment vs. those who believe in work as a blessing."[6]

We need to ask, is this true? Are there really two kinds of people in the world, divided by whether they see work as a punishment or a blessing? In creating this dichotomy, Brooks has turned away from a pragmatic disagreement. He has created, instead, a specious philosophical chasm between opposing ideological camps. This is the kind of argument Daniel Kahneman called angry science ("a summary caricature of the target position, refute the weakest argument in that caricature and declare the total destruction of the adversary's position"). There is almost no effort to find value in different points of view. There is no dialogue, only debate. Common ground has been washed away.

Brooks' discussion also frequently relies on selective, one-sided presentation of facts. This may be the most common form of unproductive argument in our current politics. Brooks writes, for example, that conservatives oppose Obama's health-care program because Obamacare is "hurting *people*" (italics in original). This is a central thesis of Brooks' political views – that liberal programs are hurting the people they are intended to help. Brooks wants to show that conservatives are not opposed to Obamacare because they are callous or indifferent, but because they *care*. He argues that Obamacare "caused millions of people to lose their doctors and their health plans...[stripped] valuable work hours away from people who are already underemployed...[and] raised premiums and deductibles of people who cannot afford to pay more."[7]

These are valid concerns. It is entirely reasonable to argue that Obamacare is a flawed program because of the facts that Brooks cites. But they are not *all* the facts. Brooks does not say that Obamacare has also provided health insurance to millions of people who previously could not afford it. Without a commitment to all the facts, we cannot have a true debate. Instead, we are talking past each other, trapped in an unproductive exchange of adversarial positions that cannot be resolved.[8]

Without a commitment to consider all the facts, we are looking out over the crowd and picking out our friends.

A liberal fighter

Elizabeth Warren tells a different story of American history. Warren's story is about the creation of great wealth but also unnecessary inequality and hardship. She tells the stories of those who are struggling to provide financial stability for their families and educational opportunities for their children in an economy that overwhelmingly benefits the wealthy. This is the paradigmatic liberal narrative of the American economy.[9]

For Arthur Brooks, America's greatness is the result of our entrepreneurial creativity and our freedom to strive for success unencumbered by "a brick wall of government regulation." For Elizabeth Warren, the source of American greatness is our willingness, often against strong conservative opposition, to support workers and the middle class. For Brooks, our current problems stem from policies and programs that lead to stagnation and dependence instead of enterprise and wealth. For Warren, our current problems are caused by greed, racial injustice, and the political influence of a wealthy few. Both of these narratives, of course, may, in some respects, be true.

Despite these different ideologies, it may still be possible to find common ground. There are opportunities, even in these impassioned manifestos, for shared concerns and a pragmatic debate.

Brooks and Warren are both concerned about a decline in social mobility in modern America and a loss of jobs that can support a family. Brooks acknowledges that social mobility is possible far less often now than in previous generations, and that "the ladder of economic opportunity seems to be missing its lowest rungs."[10] On this issue, there is both a shared goal and some agreement on basic facts. There is less agreement on the causes of this problem and its solution. But, for creating common ground, we are already several steps forward.

There are other shared concerns. Both Brooks and Warren are concerned about the decline in academic achievement of American students and that the cost of a college education is prohibitive for many families; both are also concerned about the financial insecurity of many Americans and the increasing cost of health care.

What is missing is the possibility that the other side might have something to bring to the conversation and that a novel solution might emerge – not just a transactional compromise in which each side gives up some of what they want, but a compromise that acknowledges each person's legitimate concerns and incorporates the best ideas from different points of view. The good news is that, in some instances (often behind the scenes) these kinds of discussions are taking place, and some political leaders may be more open to collaborative problem-solving than their partisan rhetoric suggests.

Pragmatic liberalism

Contemporary essayist Adam Gopnik has presented an understanding of liberalism that may also help us come closer together. Gopnik offers answers to the questions we began with – what is the essence of political liberalism and conservatism? He argues that liberal policies "all have as their end eliminating cruelty and sadism and needless suffering from the world." Humane reform of punishments and prisons, the abolition of slavery, equal rights for women, and making public services open to all people emanate from this core liberal ideal. In Gopnik's understanding, liberalism also includes a commitment to reasoned discussion, gradual change, and "an instinct about human conduct rooted in a rueful admission of our own fallibility."

Gopnik also acknowledges the limitations of liberal ideas. He writes, "the primary argument [against liberalism] is simple and compelling: the most important need humans have is for *order*... not only in their daily lives but in their world. Without order, every-thing collapses (italics in original)."[11] This is an important critique of liberalism from a passionate liberal. As an example of this con-cern, Gopnik cites Shakespeare, who, living in an era of civil and religious wars, hated tyranny but also hated anarchy and strife. In Gopnik's analysis, understanding the limits of liberalism – the need for order in society – is what distinguishes liberalism from the extreme left.

Gopnik then identifies what he considers *bad* liberal ideas, espe-cially, "a fatal over-reliance on reason [and] the chaos that could follow from the belief that society should be remade all at once on the basis of a big idea, with tradition and custom annihilated."[12] He lists several other bad liberal ideas: secularism (an intoler-ance toward religious faith), cosmopolitanism (an indifference to national loyalty), permissiveness (disdain for simple moral ideas), and excessive moral relativism, all of which undermine the positive value of tradition in people's lives.

Gopnik's acknowledgment of the limits of liberalism is an example of intellectual humility and an important step toward mutual understanding. Andrew Sullivan, writing in defense of con-servatism, shares many of these concerns.

The conservative soul

Sullivan begins his book, *The Conservative Soul*, with an evocative statement: "All conservatism begins with loss." In a recent inter-view, Sullivan defined conservatism as,

> a defense of what is, a love of what you already have, a fear that it could disappear, a sense of the fragility of the world, and the importance of being pragmatic...not having some ideological abstraction you want to force on reality, but understanding reality as something that can give you occasions for change, which we do need, but also warnings for excessive change and excessive radicalism.[13]

I would note, in Sullivan's understanding, the primacy of emotions – love (of what you already have), fear (of radical change), and loss. Resentment and hatred have no place in Sullivan's conservative politics.

Sullivan distinguishes conservatism from fundamentalism. He argues that fundamentalism is a corruption of conservatism and, in many ways, the antithesis of conservatism. He wants to rescue true conservatism from the fundamentalism, both secular and religious, that he believes (already in 2006, when his book was published) has taken over political conservatism in America.

Fundamentalism, in Sullivan's analysis, is characterized by certainty and absolutism. For the fundamentalist, "there is *no more gray*" (italics in original). In the fundamentalist mindset, certainty replaces doubt, and truth is "revealed and unified." Fundamentalists see themselves as part of a cosmic struggle; they believe that we need to protect ourselves from evil and that their opponents are agents of evil. (Sullivan notes, "there is a Satan, somewhere" in every fundamentalist ideology.) Fundamentalism requires a surrender to authority that extends to all aspects and details of daily life. Fundamentalist movements are also "invariably led by men" and "the roles of men and women are clearly marked."

True conservatism, in Sullivan's view, is based not on certainty, but on doubt. A conservative is defined by his "profound grasp of the limits of human understanding." "A conservative," Sullivan writes, is doubtful of "most ideas for 'improving' humankind, 'solving' pressing problems, 'ending' inequality, ridding the world of tyranny, 'protecting the children' and other well-meaning abstractions."[14]

Both Gopnik and Sullivan consider doubt and fallibility to be core principles of their different political philosophies. They may mean different things by fallibility, but there is, in this case, the possibility of common ground – a rejection of fundamentalism and ideological extremism, and a movement toward intellectual humility and pragmatic solutions.

Sullivan ends his book with a statement of policies a conservative will be likely to support. A conservative will resist regulations and higher taxes (because they restrict individual liberty), especially progressive taxation. Unlike libertarians, a conservative will support some efforts to ameliorate poverty and help those experiencing hardship. For example, a conservative will support free public schools until age 18 (without which, Sullivan acknowledges, his own education would have been impossible). He believes that government should "provide access to basic health care for the indigent (but no more)" as well as "clean air and safe streets...roads...etc." A conservative will want to preserve traditions; unlike the fundamentalist, however, she recognizes that "tradition is not a static entity. Although conservatism leans toward regretting change and loss, it is not wedded to the past."[15] She accepts and even celebrates social change that begins from the bottom up, rather than imposed from the top down, based on the opinions of experts who presume to know the truth.

Sullivan acknowledges that there is some irony in his arguments – that the society he loves and wants to preserve, a society of freedom and pluralism, is, to a great extent, an achievement of liberalism.

There are, of course, many objections that can be raised in response to Sullivan's analysis and policy proposals. A liberal is likely to question Sullivan's understanding of social change. Liberals will point out that important social changes often occur as the result of a complex, reciprocal relationship between bottom-up and top-down processes, and that the most consequential changes in modern American history – civil rights for African Americans, women's rights, gay rights (for which Sullivan was a leading advocate), even the right to vote – did not happen only from the bottom up. They were inspired by top-down ideals for creating a more just society and required unpopular activism, followed by controversial legislation and judicial decisions.

A liberal will also disagree with Sullivan about other issues. Liberals will ask, why these government interventions and not others? Why only basic health care and no more? A liberal would especially reply that social justice is not an "abstraction," but a lived experience. Social justice is a lived experience for black citizens who receive harsher sentences than whites for the same crime and for women who receive less pay and fewer promotions for equal work.[16] Poverty is also not an abstraction.

Gopnik and Sullivan differ in their animating concerns and the policies they support. They share, however, a recognition that ideologies have intrinsic limits, and they are willing to state the limits of their beliefs.

In rejecting ideological purity, we will still disagree. But we will more often be discussing priorities, not absolute principles, and we will have moved away from certainty and dogmatism in the direction of a dialogue based on shared concerns. We will more clearly see some truth and reason on the other side, and we will be able to talk together with less disparagement and contempt.

This idea was understood a long time ago, in a galaxy far, far away. As they battle and debate, Obi-Wan Kenobi tells Anakin Skywalker, "Only a Sith deals in absolutes."

Finding common ground 14

The future of America's children

Over the past decade, a consensus has emerged about a core problem of contemporary American society. By almost all accounts, American families and America's children are not doing well. Children in poor and working-class families, in both rural and inner-city communities, are doing especially poorly. Over the past several decades, we have experienced a decline in our national health that other countries have not, a decline in our educational success, and a dramatic increase in deaths due to drug overdose, alcoholism, and suicide.[1]

Journalist David Leonhardt offers this description:

> For almost forty years now, the United States has been doing a worse job than any similar country of keeping its citizens healthy and alive… These trends have hit working-class Americans… much harder than white-collar professionals.
>
> The number of children living with only one parent or with neither has doubled since the 1970s. The obesity rate has nearly tripled. The number of Americans who have spent time behind bars at some point has risen five-fold. Measures of childhood mental health have deteriorated.

DOI: 10.4324/9781032679075-18

Leonhardt continues,

> Among people under age fifty, the United States is no longer the most educated country in the world. A higher share of Canadians, Australians, Japanese, South Koreans, Dutch, Irish, and British now graduate from at least a two-year college. The lack of progress among American men has been especially stark.[2]

Conservative economist Oren Cass presents this assessment:

> In the past, our society was much less affluent, and yet the typical worker could support a family. How could it be that, as we have grown wealthier as a society, we have lost the ability to make that kind of arrangement work? Or do we just not want to?[3]

When I was growing up in the 1950s and 1960s, working-class parents, usually on one income, could buy a home and support a family. This is no longer true. This fact alone tells an important story of contemporary America.

In this chapter, I will discuss proposals about how we can solve these problems, presented by writers from different points of view. The proposals are compassionate and patriotic; ambitious and pragmatic; tender-minded at their source and tough-minded when necessary. All have the potential to set in motion an upward spiral of benefits in the quality of life for American children, families, and communities. One of these long-term benefits may be less hatred and political division.

These writers pass every test of constructive dialogue and problem-solving. Although they begin with different temperaments and political philosophies, they are respectful of opposing points of view. They listen with empathy, influenced by the stories of people's lives. They are charitable in their understanding of ideas they disagree with. They look for what is constructive in any proposal to improve life in America, whether it is liberal or conservative. They are open-minded.

Each writer begins with concerns shared by most Americans – how can we reverse the decline in the health and well-being of American families? How can we help all American children grow up in conditions that offer them an opportunity to succeed and contribute to a society that has supported them and toward which they feel some measure of gratitude and pride?

The "working hypothesis"

Oren Cass notes that, although the facts about the current problems of working-class families are widely accepted, when politicians look for causes, they blame the other side. Rather than admitting the failures of their own policies (and the limits of their ideology), each party continues to believe that *their* ideas are right, and their opponents are wrong. Each side argues that if only their policies had been more fully implemented and not obstructed by the other party, we would not have these problems. This is an example, in politics, of "belief perseverance" – despite new facts, people rarely change their minds about things that matter.

Cass argues that, in many ways, we have all been wrong. He challenges the widely accepted assumption that growth in our Gross Domestic Product (GDP) is the best measure of a healthy economy. He offers an alternative vision of social and economic goals he calls, "the working hypothesis." The working hypothesis is both a statement of values and a set of proposals to help solve urgent economic and social problems. The core premise of this model is that *"a labor market in which workers can support strong families and communities is the central determinant of long-term prosperity and should be the central focus of public policy"* (italics added).[4]

Cass explains,

> Alongside stable political institutions that protect basic freedoms, family and community provide the social structures necessary to a thriving society and a growing economy. Those institutions in turn rely on a foundation of productive work through which people find purpose and satisfaction in providing

for themselves and helping others. The durable growth that produces long-term prosperity is the emergent property of a virtuous cycle in which people who are able to support their families and communities improve their own productivity and raise a subsequent generation able to accomplish even more. Conversely, without access to work that can support them, families struggle to remain intact or to form in the first place, and communities cannot help but dissolve; without stable families and communities, economic opportunity vanishes.

He continues,

The goal [of our educational system] should be to ensure that every person, no matter her starting circumstances, can find a vocation that allows her to support a family, live in a community where she can build a good life, and then give to her children even greater opportunity than she had herself.[5]

In these statements of values and goals, we are standing firmly on common ground.

Many of Cass's recommendations are controversial. He proposes a federal wage subsidy for low-income workers, but he opposes an increase in the minimum wage (which imposes additional costs on employers, often small business owners, and may adversely affect the low-wage workers it is intended to help). He recommends, in many cases, a relaxation of environmental regulations in order to incentivize and support new business investment, even at the cost of negative environmental impact. Most liberals are likely to strongly disagree with both of these proposals. Cass acknowledges their concerns and offers pragmatic reasons for the policies he supports.

Cass also recommends an expansion of vocational training and apprenticeship programs, beginning in high school, to replace what he believes is the idealistic, but impractical goal of college for all students. He notes that the vocational/apprenticeship model is common in all other developed countries and highly successful. ("Germany's apprenticeship system offers recognized qualifications in 350 occupations, and 80 percent of its young adults are employed within six months of completing their education, compared with 48 percent in the United States.")[6] These programs have also been successful when tried in the United States. In Cass's model, a vocational/apprenticeship track would be voluntary, not based on a high-pressure exam. He argues that, in America, we have created a single track educational system that favors people who are likely to succeed anyway.

Cass's proposals are a model of pragmatism. On every issue, he evaluates what has been successful and what has failed and what the short-term and long-term effects of any policy are likely to be. His analysis and recommendations are based on the principles that every policy will have multiple effects, and that costs are often difficult to measure. It is well beyond my expertise to evaluate the data presented by Cass in support of these recommendations, and experts have challenged many of his proposals. But this is a different kind of discussion, the beginning of a constructive debate, the kind of discussion we need.

Our opportunity gap

In the early 2010s, political scientist Robert Putnam returned to his hometown of Port Clinton, Ohio and other representative places in America to study the lives of American children. Putnam graduated from high school in 1959. He describes Port Clinton, then and now.

> In Port Clinton of the 1950s, the children of manual workers and of professionals came from similar homes and mixed unselfconsciously in schools and neighborhoods, in scout troops and church groups ... affluent kids and poor kids lived near each other, played and prayed together, and even dated one another... Virtually everyone in the PCHS [Port Clinton High School] class of 1959, whatever their background, lived with two parents, in homes their parents owned, and in neighborhoods where everyone knew everyone else's first name.

> Nowadays, by contrast, fewer and fewer of us, in Port Clinton and elsewhere, are exposed in our daily lives to people outside

our own socioeconomic niche. Port Clinton today is a place of stark class divisions, where (according to school officials) wealthy kids park BMW convertibles in the high school lot next to decrepit junkers that homeless classmates drive away each night to live in.[7]

Almost all Americans believe in the goal of equality of opportunity. Over the past half-century, we have moved farther away from this goal. The support available to affluent kids, beginning in the first weeks of life and continuing throughout childhood, is dramatically different from the support available to poor and working-class children. Differences in family and community resources have created an increasing "opportunity gap" for children in America.

Poor kids experience fewer responsive adult interactions and more frequent Adverse Childhood Experiences. Affluent kids live in neighborhoods that collectively support children and teens. Putnam documents that the neighborhoods we live in, independent of our individual talents and the support of our families, have significant effects on children's educational success. This is true in both cities and rural areas.

Affluent kids attend safer schools where teachers have more time and energy to teach, not simply maintain order. Their schools offer more extracurricular activities (and their parents can afford the fees required). They are more likely to find mentors to support and guide them through periods of uncertainty and discouragement.

The disadvantages of poor children are cumulative. A poor kid has much less chance of graduating from college than a similarly competent and talented rich kid. Social class is a better predictor than test scores of whether an eighth grader will graduate from college.[8]

At about the same time that Putnam was visiting Port Clinton, journalist Nicholas Kristof and his wife, Sheryl WuDunn, returned to the rural community of Yamhill, Oregon, where Kristof had grown up in the 1960s. Kristof and WuDunn tell the stories of Nick's elementary and high school classmates who rode the bus with him to school and their subsequent lives of failure, drug addiction, crime, and suicide.

Kristof and WuDunn believe that Yamhill is a microcosm of rural America. They report a deeply disheartening picture of the health and conditions of life for large segments of American society:

> "...working-class communities have collapsed into a miasma of unemployment, broken families, drugs, obesity and early death. America created the first truly middle-class society in the world, but now a large share of Americans feel themselves at risk of tumbling out of that security and comfort. There's a brittleness to life for about *150 million Americans* (italics added) with a constant risk that sickness, layoffs or a car accident will cause everything to collapse.[9]

Other wealthy countries have these problems far less than we do. The United States has thirteen million children living in poverty and many children living in extreme poverty (equivalent to poverty in Congo or Bangladesh). Extreme child poverty is rare in other developed countries. There is almost no extreme child poverty in Germany

In both Port Clinton and Yamhill, the immediate cause of this social decline was the closing of businesses that had provided employment – jobs that had supported a stable family life, savings for children's education, a feeling of belonging and pride, and hopefulness for the future. Putnam writes, "In every movement of this composition the deep, throbbing, ominous bass line has been the steady deterioration of the economic circumstances of lower-class families, especially compared to the expanding resources available to upper-class parents."[10]

In this assessment of contemporary American society, we are, again, firmly on common ground, based on a concern shared by most Americans.

Our ultimate "purple" problem

Putnam calls the opportunity gap between poor and affluent kids America's "ultimate 'purple' problem." The gap is present in both red and blue states. Some causes can be seen better through a "conservative" lens of changing cultural attitudes (for example, about premarital births) and others through a "liberal" lens (for example, increasing income inequality). Putnam argues that we need to "reach across boundaries of party and ideology" and consider "the full spectrum of potential solutions."

Putnam argues persuasively that a child's success in life depends on the presence of ongoing support – stepping-stones – at every stage of development and with each new challenge she encounters. Kids rely, throughout childhood and adolescence, on the knowledge, resources, and encouragement provided by parents, teachers, coaches, and mentors. We need policies that put back in place the stepping-stones to success that have been removed by economic and social changes over the past several decades.

These facts force us to reconsider the concept of equality "at the starting line not the finish line," often used to describe a conservative approach to the problem of social inequality. This distinction now becomes almost meaningless. For kids to be successful, they need support all along the way.

Those of us who grew up in a different time, when neighborhood and community supports were more widespread, often take this support for granted. Putnam tells us,

> Before I began this research, I was like that. I've worked hard, I thought, to rise from a modest background in Port Clinton - much of the time heedless of how much my good fortune depended on family and community and public institutions in that more communitarian and egalitarian age. If I and my classmates could climb the ladder, so could kids from modest backgrounds today. Having finished this research, I know better.[11]

Putnam believes that the solution begins with policies to revive a stagnant working-class economy. A "sustained economic revival for low-paid workers would be as close to a magic bullet" as we have to arrest the vicious cycle of social breakdown he has extensively documented.

At the same time as we pursue policies of economic revival, there is much more that we can do. Putnam is a pragmatist. He presents recommendations to improve opportunities for poor children in the short term, based on his assessment of the best evidence available. We have some knowledge of which programs are most likely to be effective. We also have some knowledge of how much (or how little) successful programs cost and how much these investments are likely to save our society over the long term.

Putnam reports that small amounts of additional cash for poor families (proposed in different forms by both liberals and conservatives) result in improved academic achievements for their children, "especially if the funds are concentrated on the child's earliest years." He cites the need to reduce incarceration for non-violent offenses, which destroys families, and he recommends increased workplace flexibility and parental leave. "Virtually all other advanced countries provide much more support for parents (especially low-income parents) during their children's first year of life than we do."[12]

Putnam believes that the solution will also require improved parent education, beginning early in a child's life, and increased investment in early childhood education. Professional parent coaching by early childhood professionals, with regular home visits (for example, the Nurse-Family partnership), has demonstrated success. Preschool programs also have demonstrated success, and the essential components of the most successful programs have been identified.

Improving educational outcomes is not a red-state or blue-state issue. Oklahoma began a statewide early education program in 1998. By 2012, this program, which includes support for parents, was offered in 99% of Oklahoma school districts. Initial evaluations showed "remarkable gains in reading, writing, and math skills."[13]

Other programs, in America and other countries, using a school-community approach have been successful. In this model, health and social services are provided in the school, with youth activities offered at all hours. Parents and community members are encouraged to engage in the educational process. The Harlem Children's Zone (HCZ), a highly successful program founded in 1970, is an example of this approach. HCZ includes early childhood programs, after-school tutoring and extracurricular activities, and other supports for children and families. HCZ Promise Academy, the organization's flagship school, "has made major progress in closing the racial achievement gap" in NYC.

Putnam recommends, based on research, increased investment in schools, especially in poor communities; moving poor kids to new neighborhoods; and higher teacher pay. He recommends much more widely available mentoring and an end to the pay-to-play system now present in half of American high schools. Pay-to-play requires fees for students to participate in extracurricular activities. These fees often prevent poor children from joining activities that have been a road to success for many kids. Putnam notes that America invented extracurricular activities.

Putnam also endorses expanded vocational and apprenticeship education. This recommendation is supported by both liberals and conservatives. Oren Cass, Arthur C. Brooks, Nicholas Kristof and Sheryl WuDunn, and many others share this conclusion. Putnam reports that "the United States spends (as a fraction of our economy) roughly one tenth as much...as other countries" on vocational and apprenticeship programs.[14]

A national commission on the American family

In these three studies of American society, we have a wealth of proposals to improve the health of American families and opportunities for American children. *Our Kids* should be required reading for anyone concerned about the future of America. The proposals presented by Putnam, Kristof and WuDunn, and Cass are supported by research on both benefits and costs. The benefits are great, and the costs are often low.

The scope and urgency of these problems require a national commitment. Again, this is not a red-state or a blue-state problem.

It is not a rural or an inner-city problem. The lives of 150 million Americans are affected by financial insecurity.

This may be our best opportunity to put aside partisanship and significantly improve the lives of Americans across the country – to rebuild communities, enhance the physical and emotional health of large numbers of citizens, restore hope and pride, increase the chance for all children to move from poverty to success, re-establish the pre-eminence of our educational system, and allow many more Americans to find meaningful connections with others.

Establishing a consensus on specific initiatives should be the work of a national commission. Much of the research on how to create a better future for our children has already been done. Our political leaders now need to make this happen.

Notes

Introduction

1. Edsall, T. *No Hate Left Behind*. New York Times, March 13, 2019. In 1960, 4% of Democrats and 5% of Republicans did not want their children to marry someone from the opposing party. In 2010, 33% of Democrats and 49% of Republicans felt this way! This disheartening change took place during a time when acceptance of other forms of intermarriage – between different religions, racial groups, and the marriage of same-sex couples – dramatically increased. Putnam, R. (2020). *The Upswing: How America Came Together a Century Ago and How We Can Do It Again*. Simon and Schuster, p. 98.
2. Finkel, E. J., et al. (October 30, 2020). Political Sectarianism in America. *Science*, 370: 6516, p. 533
3. Krugman, P. *Good Economy, Negative Vibes: The Story Continues*. New York Times, April 8, 2024.
4. Cohen, G. (2022). *Belonging: The Science of Creating Connections and Bridging Divides*. Norton.
5. Finkel, E. J. et al. (2002), p. 534.
6. Putnam, R. (2020). Here are some examples: Putnam reports, "In 1950, 12% of students agreed with the statement, 'I am a very important person.' By 1990, that figure had risen to 80%!" We now use the word "I" much more often. "The frequency of the word 'I' in all American books ... doubled between 1965 and 2008." We more

often choose uncommon names for our children, an expression of the importance we place of individuality and the need to "stand out" vs. common names, which suggest the importance of community and a desire to "fit in."

7. Hochschild, A. R. (2016). *Strangers in Their Own Land: Anger and Mourning on the American Right.* The New Press, p. 5.

8. There are exceptions, of course, to this ideological consistency; we may be conservative on one issue and liberal on others. Political partisans, however, are remarkably consistent, perhaps now more than ever.

    Some political scientists have argued for a pluralistic understanding of modern politics. From this perspective, what we call liberalism and conservatism are not coherent ideologies, but, instead, coalitions of convenience among disparate political philosophies and interest groups. In some ways, the pluralist perspective must be correct. There are important differences (and, at times, schisms) within both liberal and conservative schools of thought. Most scholars, however, accept a liberal – conservative distinction as a meaningful way of understanding our political differences.

    Psychologist Sylvan Tomkins (1995) offered a helpful analogy. Tomkins compared ideologies to families; ideologies are families of ideas. Following Tomkins' metaphor, different forms of liberalism and conservatism are siblings or cousins. They are different but share important characteristics and a common parentage or grandparentage.

9. The analogies of deep grammar and theme and variations are used by Corey Robin in Robin, C. (2018). *The Reactionary Mind: Conservatism from Edmund Burke to Donald Trump.* Oxford University Press.

10. Will, G. (2019). *The Conservative Sensibility.* Hachette Books.

11. Sowell, T. (2007). *A Conflict of Visions: Ideological Origins of Political Struggles, Revised ed.* Basic Books.

12. James, W. (1907/2000). *Pragmatism and Other Writings.* Penguin Classics.

13. Tomkins, S. S. (1995). *Exploring Affect: The Selected Writings of Sylvan S. Tomkins* (Ed. E. Virginia Demos). Cambridge University Press.

14. Lakoff, G. (2009). *The Political Mind.* Penguin.

15. Haidt, J. (2012). *The Righteous Mind: Why Good People Are Divided by Politics and Religion.* Pantheon.

16. Hibbing, J. R., Smith, K. B., & Alford, J. R. (2014). *Predisposed: Liberals, Conservatives, and the Biology of Political Differences*. Routledge.
17. Hetherington, M., & Weiler, J. (2018). *Prius or Pickup: How the Answers to Four Simple Questions Explain America's Great Divide*. Houghton Mifflin Harcourt.
18. Hunter, J. D. (1991). *Culture Wars: The Struggle to Define America*. Basic Books
19. Robin, C. 2018.
20. Kahneman, D. (2023). *Adversarial Collaboration. An EDGE Lecture*. https://www.edge.org/adversarial-collaboration-daniel-kahneman
21. Studies of confirmation bias are discussed in Cohen, G. (2022), pp. 288–299.
22. Gilovich, T., & Ross, L. (2015). *The Wisest One in the Room: How You Can Benefit from Social Psychology's Most Powerful Insights*. Free Press. See also Mascolo, M. F. (2024). Toward a More Collaborative Democracy: Bridging Political Divides through Dialectical Problem-Solving. In N. Shannon, M. F. Mascolo, and A. Belolutskaya (Eds.). *Routledge International Handbook of Dialectical Thinking*, Routledge, pp. 353–373.

Chapter 1: Liberal and conservative: A brief history

1 Hibbing, J. R., Smith, K. B., & Alford, J. R. (2014).
2 Russell, B. (1945/2007). *A History of Western Philosophy*. Touchstone, p. xxiii.
3 Allitt, P. (2009). *The Conservative Tradition*. The Teaching Company.
4 Gopnik, A. (2019). *A Thousand Small Sanities: The Moral Adventure of Liberalism*. Basic Books.
5 Russell, B. (1945/2007), p. 597.
   In Russell's account, philosophical and political liberalism originated in England and Holland as a movement for religious tolerance. Liberals were Protestants (but not fanatical Protestants). They "regarded religious wars as silly," supported democracy and the middle class rather than the aristocracy, favored restrictions on the role of heredity, and opposed the divine right of kings. Liberal ideas found their most well-known expression in the philosophy of John Locke and later, John Stuart Mill.
6 Gopnik, A. 2019, pp. 18, 83.
7 Scruton, R. (2017). *Conservatism: An Introduction to the Great Tradition*. All Points Books.

8 James, W. (1907/2000), p. 11.
9 Tomkins, S. S. (1995).

Beginning with this basic difference, Tomkins identified additional characteristics of ideological polarities; for example, that man is an end in himself vs. man is not an end in himself; that man is basically good vs. man is basically evil; that "man should be the object of love vs. man should be loved if he is worthy"; and that "man should be the object of respect vs. man should be respected if he is respectable."

Tomkins writes, "Nowhere is the polarity between the left and the right sharper than in the attitudes towards man's affects. The left...is at home in the realm of feeling. The right is uneasy about and intolerant of affect per se, lest it endanger norm attainment." Echoes of Tomkins' polarities can be found in more recent ideas, especially George Lakoff's nurturant parent and strict father moralities.

A series of recent studies in both the United States and Sweden found support for Tomkins' theory. The polarity of humanism vs. normativism was strongly predictive of liberal and conservative political beliefs. Nilsson, A., & Jost, J. T. (2020). *Rediscovering Tomkins' Polarity Theory: Humanism, Normativism, and the Psychological Basis of Left-Right Ideological Conflict in the U.S. and Sweden.* PLOS ONE, 15(7):e0236627.

10 Sowell, T. (2007), pp. 34, 243.

Sowell's theory of visions, however, leaves important questions unanswered, especially the question of "why?" Where does a vision originate? Sowell argues that visions are not derived from different "value premises" and they are not rationalizations of self-interest or a justification for the status quo. He cites writers with a constrained vision who supported social change, often at personal risk, including James Madison and Alexander Hamilton. These examples, however, may be exceptions. In almost all cases, the constrained vision accepts the current social order as a source of stability and wisdom, and regards most direct efforts to achieve a more just society as foolish or dangerous.

I would note some irony in Sowell's ideas. *A Conflict of Visions* is a scholarly and balanced book, presenting both visions in a charitable way. In Sowell's writing for the general public, however, balance and intellectual charity are hard to find. Sowell is consistently disdainful and dismissive of policies based on an unconstrained vision; he writes contemptuously, for example, about supporters of gun control and efforts to reduce global warming.

11 Lakoff, G. (2009).

12 Baumrind, D. (1989). Rearing Competent Children. In W. Damon (Ed.). *Child Development Today and Tomorrow.* Jossey-Bass.

13 Haidt, J. (2012), p. 44, italics in original.

14 A morality of Care is derived from the need to protect and care for children. This moral foundation "makes us sensitive to signs of suffering and need; it makes us despise cruelty and want to care for those who are suffering." A morality of Fairness evolved from our need to form partnerships and work collaboratively with non-kin. This moral foundation leads to a concern with equality and justice. The moral foundation of Loyalty evolved from our need to form coalitions to compete with other human groups. When this moral foundation is active, we are alert to evidence of betrayal and develop a hatred of traitors. A morality of Authority evolved because of the advantage to group survival conferred by social hierarchies. The moral foundation of Sanctity is derived from the need to protect ourselves from infection by pathogens, experienced as feelings of disgust. The emotion of disgust remains active as a moral intuition; physical disgust becomes moral disgust. (For example, we describe both rotten food and rotten people as disgusting.) Haidt argues that disgust is the origin of our xenophobia and exclusion of others, but also our ideals of purity and sacredness, values that help bind human groups and confer an important (perhaps essential) advantage to our survival. There is both a positive value and a dark side to sanctity.

I would note, however, two limitations of this model. Although Haidt identifies five distinct moral foundations, the foundations of Care and Fairness are highly correlated, as are the foundations of Loyalty, Authority, and Purity. Liberals in Haidt's research are likely to endorse a morality of both Care and Fairness. Conservatives who use the moral foundation of Loyalty are also likely to feel strongly about the importance of Authority and Sanctity. These correlations suggest a more parsimonious explanation that reduces our moral foundations to two basic sources of moral intuition and reasoning.

It is also possible that the conservative advantage is less of a real-life advantage than Haidt believes. Although conservatives endorse all five moral foundations in research questionnaires, a historical perspective does not support an important role for Care and Fairness in conservative political philosophy or the policies of most conservative governments. There is a plausible alternative. Although many conservatives genuinely believe in compassion and fairness, the values of loyalty, authority, and purity may take priority in their political choices.

15 Hibbing, J. R., Smith, K. B., & Alford, J. R. (2014).

16 Tuschman, A. (2013). *Our Political Nature: The Evolutionary Origins of What Divides Us.* Prometheus Books.

Tuschman begins with evidence that political attitudes are strongly influenced by genetics and are highly stable from early childhood. In a frequently cited study, researchers found that observations of children's temperaments recorded by their preschool teachers predicted political attitudes as young adults. Conservative young adults had been described when they were preschoolers as "uncomfortable with uncertainty," "rigidifying when experiencing duress," and "relatively over-controlled." The girls were described as "quiet, neat, compliant, fearful, tearful…and hoped for help from the adults around." Preschoolers who identified as liberals as young adults were described as more "autonomous, expressive, energetic, and relatively under-controlled." "Liberal girls had higher levels of self-assertiveness, talkativeness, curiosity, and openness to expressing negative feelings" (p. 24).

Tuschman reports additional evidence that biological differences may contribute to differences in political opinions. Student volunteers at University College London who identified themselves as conservative showed a larger amygdala (a brain structure responsible for processing fear and aggression); students who described themselves as liberal showed a larger anterior cingulate (involved in higher-level functions, including attention and decision-making). These differences in brain structure were able to accurately predict a student's political orientation 72% of the time, and these results have been replicated (p. 31).

Correlations of this magnitude are highly significant for social science research. But, of course, predictions based on brain structure are inaccurate 28% of the time, and they are still only correlations.

Tuschman reports some additional intriguing findings: Climate has some influence on political attitudes. People who live closer to the equator tend to be more conservative; people who live farther from the equator tend to be more liberal. When people move to a different climate, their political attitudes usually correspond to the environment of their ancestors, not where they currently live (p. 30).

17 Hibbing, J. R., Smith, K. B., & Alford, J. R. (2014), p. 94.

18 Hetherington, M., & Weiler, J. (2018).

19 Jost, J. T., Federico, C. M., & Napier, J. L. (2009). Political Ideology: Its Structure, Functions, and Elective Affinities. *Annual Review of Psychology*, 60:307–37.
20 Hetherington, M., & Weiler, J. (2018), pp. 3, 4, 14, 15.

Chapter 2: Beyond politics: The essence of liberalism and conservatism

1 Solomon, A. *My Book Was Censored in China. Now It's Blacklisted – in Texas.* NY Times, November 23, 2021.
2 Volkan, V. (1997). *Blood Lines: From Ethnic Pride to Ethnic Cleansing.* Westview Press.
3 Sulloway, F. J. (1996). *Born to Rebel: Birth Order, Family Dynamics, and Creative Lives.* Vintage Books.

In my own field of psychoanalysis, a generation of conservative ("classical") psychoanalysts, many of whom were liberal, even radical, in their political beliefs, established a conservative hegemony in psychoanalysis. Innovations in theory and therapeutic practice were regarded as a threat to the integrity of psychoanalysis. Classical psychoanalysis defended an orthodoxy of ideas, with ritualized in-group membership and out-group exclusion. For at least a generation, adherence to core ideas and therapeutic procedures (the theory of instinctual drives and therapeutic principles of abstinence and neutrality) became a shibboleth separating "true" psychoanalysis from "non-analytic" innovations. From the classical perspective, modifications of psychoanalytic theory and practice were something else, not psychoanalysis.

4 University of Michigan. *Study: Evolution Now Accepted by Majority of Americans.* Michigan News, August 20, 2021.
5 McCarten, A. (2019). *The Two Popes: Francis, Benedict, and the Decision that Shook the World.* Flatiron Books.
6 For a discussion of the papacy of Pope Francis from this perspective, see Douthat, R. *Can Liberal and Conservative Catholics Coexist?* New York Times, May 8, 2024.
7 Goldwater, B. (1960/2011). *The Conscience of a Conservative.* Martino Fine Books.
8 Lakoff, G. (2009), p. 47.
9 Gopnik, A. (2019).
10 An extensive body of research supports the role of fear in conservative political attitudes. When we are reminded of our mortality, we become more conservative. For example, when people are asked

to read passages that evoke a fear of death, they are more likely to support harsher punishments for criminals; they express more positive evaluations of those who praise their culture and religion (and more negative evaluations of those who criticize it); they express greater support for traditional gender norms; and they are more likely to support violent solutions to ethnic, religious, and international conflicts. Pyszczynski, T., Solomon, S., & Greenberg, J. (2015). Thirty Years of Terror Management Theory: From Genesis to Revelation. *Advances in Experimental Social Psychology, 52*:1–70.

11 Volkan, V. (1994). *The Need to Have Enemies and Allies: From Clinical Practice to International Relationships.* Jason Aronson.

12 Will, G. (2019).

13 Levin, Y. (2014). *The Great Debate: Edmund Burke, Thomas Paine, and the Birth of Right and Left.* Basic Books.

14 Tuschman, A. (2013), p. 69.

15 Tuschman, A. (2013), p. 67.

16 Political psychologist John Jost and colleagues refer to these as the "motivational substructure" and "discursive superstructure" of political ideology. Jost, J. T., Federico, C.M., & Napier, J.L. (2009).

17 Levin, Y. (2014).

Chapter 3: Political emotions: The politics of resentment, humiliation, pride, and fear

1 Lukianoff, G., & Haidt, J. (2018). *The Coddling of The American Mind: How Good Intentions and Bad Ideas are Setting Up a Generation for Failure.* Penguin Books.

2 Fukuyama, F. (2018). *Identity: The Demand for Dignity and The Politics of Resentment.* Farrar, Strauss, Giroux.

Other scholars agree. In his classic study of the origins of war from ancient Greece through the Cold War, historian Donald Kagan observed: "how small a role considerations of practical utility and material gain, and even ambition for power itself, play in bringing on wars, and how often some aspect of honor is decisive." (Kagan, D., 1995. *On the Origins of War.* Doubleday, p. 8.) More recently, Adam Gopnik notes that "identity or national pride…has proven time and again to be incomparably more powerful than economic self-interest." Gopnik cites, for example, Benjamin Disraeli's insight that "an appeal to national grandeur would be wildly popular"among the newly enfranchised working class in Britain. (Gopnik, A., 2019, p. 94.)

3 Fukuyama, F. (2018), pp. 7–8.

Fukuyama could have added many other examples of the importance of dignity and pride, in politics and in our everyday lives. Some expressions of pride are universal and (usually) benign; others are costly; some, in their everyday forms, are healthy but can quickly turn hateful and malignant. We all take pride in the achievements of our children and our social groups, our sports teams, and the success and heroism of people from our hometowns. College football is all about pride.

In preparation for the 2014 World Cup games, Brazil is reported to have spent $550 million to build a soccer stadium that will be rarely used, in an effort to promote national pride. Many Brazilians thought this money could have been better spent.

4 This trend may have begun decades earlier. See David Leonhardt's recent history, *Ours Was the Shining Future: The Story of the American Dream*. Random House.

5 Cramer, K. (2016). *The Politics of Resentment: Rural Consciousness in Wisconsin and the Rise of Scott Walker*. University of Chicago Press, p. 211.

6 Hochschild, A. R. (2016).

7 Fukuyama, F. (2018), pp. 59–73.

8 Sandel, M. J. (2020). *The Tyranny of Merit: What's Become of the Common Good*. Farrar, Strauss and Giroux.

9 Case, A., & Deaton, A. (2020). *Deaths of Despair and the Future of Capitalism*. Princeton University Press, pp. 7–8.

10 Sandel, M. J. (2020), p. 26.

11 Tangney, J. P., & Fischer, K. W. (Eds.). (1995). *Self-Conscious Emotions: The Psychology of Shame, Guilt, Embarrassment, and Pride*. New York: The Guilford Press.

12 Scheff, T. J., & Ratzinger, S. M. (1991). *Emotions and Violence: Shame and Rage in Destructive Conflicts*. Authors Guild Backinprint.com.

Psychiatrist James Gilligan, based on extensive interviews with violent criminals, has argued that "the basic psychological motive, or cause, of violent behavior is the wish to ward off or eliminate the feeling of shame and humiliation…and replace it with its opposite, the feeling of pride." Gilligan believes that shame "is the pathogen that causes violence just as specifically as the tubercle bacillus causes tuberculosis, except that in the case of violence it is an emotion, not a microbe." Gilligan, J. (2003). Shame, Guilt, and Violence. *Social Research*, 70(4):1149–1180.

13 Sandel, M. J. (2020), pp. 221–222.

14 Sandel, M. J. (2020), p. 212.

15 Murthy, V. H. (2020). *Together: Loneliness, Health, and What Happens When We Find Connection.* HarperCollins. See also Putnam, R. (2001). *Bowling Alone: The Collapse and Revival of American Community.* Simon and Shuster.

16 Hawkins, S., Yudkin, D., Juan-Torres, M., & Dixon, T. (2018). *Hidden Tribes: A Study of America's Polarized Landscape.* More in Common: www.moreincommon.com.

17 Nussbaum, M. (2018). *The Monarchy of Fear: A Philosopher Looks at Our Political Crisis.* Simon and Schuster. See also Nussbaum, M. (2004). *Hiding From Humanity: Disgust, Shame, and the Law.* Princeton University Press.

18 This is especially the case in those with an authoritarian predisposition. See Stenner, K. (2005). *The Authoritarian Dynamic.* Cambridge University Press.

19 Nussbaum reminds us of recent examples of astonishingly rapid "cascades" and "ethnification" of fear – between Muslims and Hindus in India, in the Rwanda genocide, and ethnic cleansing in the Balkans. In these horrific events, members of different groups who had lived peacefully together and intermarried began mass killings of their former friends and neighbors.

Remarkably similar events have been observed in non-human primates. Primatologist Frans De Waal reports the following chilling observations: In one African reserve, a community of chimpanzees split into two factions. These chimps "had played and groomed together, reconciled after squabbles, shared meat, and lived in harmony." When the factions began to fight over territory, "shocked researchers watched as former friends literally drank one another's blood." (Nussbaum, M., 2018, p. 80).

20 Carlson, T. Tucker Carlson Tonight. Fox News, June 8, 2020.

Chapter 4: Is dialogue possible?

1 Grose, J. *"Couples Therapy," but for Politics.* New York Times, Dec. 13, 2023.

2 Drawing from Dynamic Systems theory, Coleman describes our polarized politics as an "attractor." An attractor is a pattern of events in both physical systems and human psychology that is highly resistant to change. A cancer cell is an example of an attractor in a biological system. In psychology, an attractor is a state of mind that is easy to get into but difficult to get out of. Polarized politics has become an

attractor in American society. Coleman, P. (2021). *The Way Out: How to Overcome Toxic Polarization*. Columbia University Press.

3   Heitler, S. (1993). *From Conflict to Resolution: Skills and Strategies for Individual, Couple, and Family Therapy*. W.W. Norton.

4   Mascolo, M. F. (2024).

5   Robin, C. (2018).

6   Hunter, J. D. (1991).

7   Finkel, E. J. et al. (2020), p. 536; Hawkins, S., Yudkin, D., Juan-Torres, M., & Dixon, T. (2018).

Chapter 5: A language of dignity and respect

1   Hicks, D. (2011). *Dignity: The Essential Role It Plays in Resolving Conflict*. Yale University Press.

2   Erikson, E. (1985). Pseudospeciation in the Nuclear Age. *Political Psychology*, 6:213–217. doi: 10.2307/3790901.

3   Cohen, G. (2022), p. 305.

4   Cohen, G. (2022), p. 307.
Cohen also reports a technique called "deep canvassing." The deep canvassing project, unlike other research and most of the examples described in this book, had the explicit goal of persuading voters to support laws that protect transgender people from discrimination. The canvassers, however, did not present facts and arguments in support of their cause; instead, they listened to voters' concerns and tried to foster empathy for the experience of transgender people. The canvassers asked open-ended questions (for example, "can you say more about that?") and then listened with interest. They made voters feel that their opinions mattered. Then they asked voters to watch a short video and asked, "have you ever been in a similar situation, had a similar feeling?" Almost every voter was willing to share a story. The effects of these conversations were lasting; months later, voters expressed less antagonism toward transgender people (pp. 311–313).

We should also, of course, extend the same kind of empathy to conservatives, to help liberals understand why conservatives feel the way they do. We could ask liberals, "have you ever felt that you had worked hard for many years, devoted yourself to your family and community, but did not receive the recognition and respect you deserved?"

5   Mascolo, M. F. (2024).

6   Greene, R., & Ablon, J. S. (2006). *Treating Explosive Kids*. The Guilford Press.

Chapter 6: Learn someone's personal story

1 New York Times columnist David Brooks wisely recommends that, when having conversations, we should "storify" our ideas. Brooks explains, "I no longer ask people: What do you think about that? Instead, I ask: How did you come to believe that? That gets them talking about the people and experiences that shaped their values. People are much more revealing and personal when they are telling stories. And the conversation is going to be warmer and more fun." In this instance, Brooks is talking about our personal relationships. His advice is equally true for politics. Brooks, D. *The Essential Skills for Being Human*. New York Times, Oct. 19, 2023.

2 Psychologist Michael Mascolo calls this a feeling of "deep sociality." Mascolo, M. F. (2024).

3 Cramer, K. (2016).

   Cramer tried to understand a central set of questions that emerged from these conversations. The people she met in rural communities spoke, for example, about their need for better health and dental care, and about how many people in their towns could not afford health insurance. Yet they opposed most government spending programs, including government-sponsored health-care reform, that would offer immediate practical help.

   This was a puzzle Cramer returned to often: Why would people prefer less government when they would seemingly benefit from more of it? Why would someone who was losing his teeth oppose a state health-care plan that includes dental coverage? The answer she heard most often had to do with feelings of resentment – that politicians in Madison were not listening, that government spending would require higher taxes they could not afford, and that benefits go to "them," not "us."

   Cramer explains that "them" was defined, especially, by culture – they "do not value what we value, they do not work as hard as we do, and they are actively sucking away the livelihoods we have worked so hard to create." One resident explained, "I'm paying for healthcare for people who aren't working half as hard as I am" (p. 209).

4 Cramer asks, "The trick, then, would seem to be finding some way to prevent resentment from dominating the perspectives through which people make sense of politics. The question is, what is the fix? What is the change that needs to take place to ensure that democratic

debate is fueled by something other than resentment? She offers a few recommendations to promote better understanding between urban and rural Wisconsinites: (1) an exchange program for state legislators, requiring representatives from urban districts to spend time in rural districts and vice versa; (2) an effort to make the "invisible" resources rural communities receive from the state more visible; and (3) she returns to our most basic principle: to simply spend more time listening (p. 224).

5 Hochschild, A. R. (2016), pp. 135–151.
6 Smith, S. B. (2021). *Reclaiming Patriotism in an Age of Extremes.* Yale University Press.

We can be patriotic and still be critical of our country. Patriotism does not require us to whitewash the history of America's sins. Although admitting and atoning for America's cruelties and injustices feels unpatriotic to many, Smith believes that this is characteristic of nationalism, not patriotism. Unlike nationalism, enlightened patriotism is "aspirational, deliberative, and self-questioning." We feel regret (or hatred) for the cruel actions of other countries; we feel ashamed of the cruelties of our own.

7 Chavez, L. (2009). *An Unlikely Conservative: The Transformation of an Ex-liberal.* Basic Books.
8 French, D. (2020). *Divided We Fall: America's Secession Threat and How to Restore Our Nation.* St. Matrin's Griffin. Also French, D. *One Reason the Trump Fever Won't Break.* New York Times, Oct. 1, 2023.
9 Obama, B. *Eulogy for Police Officers Killed in Dallas, Texas.* July 12, 2016.

Chapter 7: Empathy and moral imagination

1 Boylan, J. F. *Bring Moral Imagination Back in Style.* New York Times, July 22, 2016. Boylan notes that the term moral imagination was first used by Edmund Burke to describe the idea that "our ethics should transcend our personal experience and embrace the dignity of the human race." Boylan recalls, with regret, a time when "it didn't occur to me that imagining the humanity of people other than myself was my responsibility. And yet the root cause of so much grief is our failure to do just that."
2 Adam Smith understood this in his classic discussion of empathy. (Smith, in the language of the time, used the word, "sympathy",) Smith, A. (1790/2009). *The Theory of Moral Sentiments.* Penguin.

3 Zaki, J. (2020). *The War for Kindness: Building Empathy in a Fractured World*. Broadway Books.

4 Gordon, M. (2009). *Roots of Empathy: Changing the World, Child by Child*. The Experiment, LLC.

5 Baron-Cohen, S. (2011). *The Science of Evil: On Empathy and the Origins of Cruelty*. Basic Books.

6 Eisenberg, N., & Mussen, P. (1989). *The Roots of Prosocial Behavior in Children*. Cambridge University Press.

7 Yankelovich, D. (1999). *The Magic of Dialogue: Transforming Conflict into Cooperation*. Simon and Schuster.

8 Psychologist Simon Baron-Cohen offers perhaps the strongest statement of the importance of empathy in human relationships. Baron-Cohen writes that empathy is *"the most valuable resource* in our world" (italics in original) and "a universal solvent for problems in all human relationships, both personal and international." Baron-Cohen argues that human cruelty and evil are caused by an erosion of empathy (Baron-Cohen, S., 2011, pp., 157, 191.)

9 Bloom, P. (2016). *Against Empathy: The Case for Rational Compassion*. New York: HarperCollins.

10 I discuss this example in Barish, K. (2020). Review of Against Empathy: The Case for Rational Compassion, by Paul Bloom. *The Humanistic Psychologist*, Vol. 49, No. 4, 630–645. https://doi.org/10.1037/hum0000181.

11 This example comes from C. Daniel Batson et. al., discussed in Zaki, J. (2020).

12 George W. Bush, *Eulogy for Police Officers Killed in Dallas, Texas*. July 12, 2016.

13 Barack Obama, *Eulogy for Police Officers Killed in Dallas, Texas*. July 12, 2016.

14 Nguyen, J. *Governor Cox Gives Emotional Stance on Bill Targeting Transgender Youth*. ABC4.com, February 18, 2021.

Chapter 8: From debate to dialogue

1 Yankelovich, D. (1999). Yankelovich presented this model a generation ago. There are now several programs for promoting dialogue based on similar core ideas. See, for example, Peter Coleman (2021), Michael Mascolo (2024), and BraverAngels.org.

2 Kelman, H. (2017). *Resolving Deep-Rooted Conflicts: Essays on the Theory and Practice of Interactive Problem-Solving* (Ed. W. Wintersteiner & W. Graf). Routledge. Kelman continues, "Optimism…is part of a strategy designed to create self-fulfilling prophecies of a positive nature, balancing the self-fulfilling prophecies of escalation created by pessimistic expectations and the worst-case scenarios often favoured by more traditional analysts" (p. 13).

3 Nussbaum, M. (2018).

4 Kessler, D. (2017) *Capture: Unraveling the Mystery of Mental Suffering.* HarperCollins.

5 Allport, G. (1954/1979). *The Nature of Prejudice.* Addison Wesley.

6 For a review of research, see Ramiah, A. A., & Hewstone, M. (2013). Intergroup Contact as a Tool for Reducing, Resolving, and Preventing Intergroup Conflict. *American Psychologist,* 68(7): 527–542. doi: 10.1037/a0032603

7 Time Magazine, *Essay: The Homosexual in America.* January 21, 1966.

8 Nussbaum makes a similar observation. Amy Chua recalls a comment by Ruth Bader Ginsburg, "Once [gay] people began to say who they were…you found that it was your next-door neighbor or it could be your child, and we found people we admired." Chua, A. (2019). *Political Tribes: Group Instinct and the Fate of Nations.* Penguin.

9 Nussbaum also recommends the study of philosophy as a practice of hope, exemplified by Socrates. She explains that philosophy is "not about authoritative pronouncements, but about a commitment to make arguments that are rigorous, reciprocal, and sincere, and a *willingness to listen to others as equal participants and to respond to what they offer*" (italics added). "Philosophy does not compel, threaten, or mock." "Socratic reasoning is a practice of hope because it creates a world of listening, of quiet voices, and of mutual respect for reason."

10 Holloway, J. *To Unite a Divided America, Make People Work for It.* New York Times, July 2, 2021.

11 Nussbaum, M. (2018), pp. 241–242. Sandel, M. (2020). Reich, R. B. (2018). *The Common Good.* Knopf.

12 Pink, D. H. (2018). *When: The Scientific Secrets of Perfect Timing.* Riverhead Books.

13 Bernstein, E. *The Science of Prayer.* Wall Street Journal, May 17, 2020.

Chapter 9: From opinions to concerns

1 Greene, R., & Ablon, J. S. (2006).
   Several other problem-solving models include this core principle. In Michael Mascolo's model (2024), people are encouraged to understand a problem from more than one perspective, to acknowledge the kernel of truth in each point of view, to translate opinions ("adversarial positions") into the concerns that gave rise to them, and to find a novel solution that addresses multiple concerns. Mascolo calls this, "the dialectical construction of novel forms of thinking through the integration of opposites." As with Yankelovich's dialogue model, the goal is not to win an argument but to find a better solution.
   George Yancy (2022) has described a model for "collaborative conversations" about racial issues based on similar principles. Herbert Kelman's Problem Solving Workshop also begins with an understanding of basic concerns. See also Consensus Building Institute (cbi.org).
2 Mascolo, M. F. (2024).

Chapter 10: Intellectual charity: What are your opponents' most reasonable arguments?

1 Gutting, G. (2015). *What Philosophy Can Do.* Norton.
2 Lukianoff, G., & Haidt, J. (2018). *The Coddling of the American Mind: How Good Intentions and Bad Ideas are Setting Up a Generation for Failure.* Penguin Books.
3 Gutting, G., (2015).
4 Fey, T. (2004). *Mean Girls* film.
5 Kennedy said, "Robert Bork's America is a land in which women would be forced into back-alley abortions, blacks would sit at segregated lunch counters, rogue police could break down citizens' doors in midnight raids, and schoolchildren could not be taught about evolution, writers and artists would be censored at the whim of the Government, and the doors of the Federal courts would be shut on the fingers of millions of citizens." Bork responded, "There was not a line in that speech that was accurate." See Nocera, J. (2011). *The Ugliness Started with Bork.* New York Times, October 21, 2011.
   Bork's description of liberalism in his book, *Slouching Towards Gomorrah* (1996) is equally uncharitable. It is difficult to find any charity (or humility) in Bork's description of liberalism.
6 Kahneman, D. (2023).

7 If intellectual charity is uncommon in science, it is even more uncommon in politics and personal relationships. If we rarely change our minds when interpreting the results of scientific experiments, how likely are we to change our vision of human nature and society, or our opinions about how we should defend our country or raise our children.

Chapter 11: Intellectual humility: What are the limits of your beliefs?

1 Several scholars have emphasized the importance of humility as an antidote to our current polarization. Lukianoff and Haidt recommend intellectual humility – an awareness that "our reasoning is so flawed, so prone to bias, that we can rarely be certain that we are right" – as an alternative to the emotional reasoning prevalent on college campuses. Martha Nussbaum recommends philosophical inquiry (exemplified by Socratic dialogue) as a form of humility. For Nussbaum, philosophy begins with an acknowledgment of how little we really understand. "The philosopher, because she is willing to make her arguments known, is humble and exposed...vulnerable to criticism." Conservative philosopher Robert George, in public conversations with liberal philosopher Cornell West, also emphasizes the importance of this form of intellectual humility.

There are several other important meanings of humility. David French encourages an even more fundamental attitude of "existential humility," derived from the Christian teaching of original sin. Existential humility requires an acknowledgment of the limits of all human wisdom and virtue. French notes that a feeling of threat often leads to certainty and erodes humility. Christian teaching, in contrast, reminds us that "the greatest threat comes from within ourselves." Humility is a central concept in other (perhaps all) religious traditions, especially, the idea of humility before God. Bertrand Russell, an atheist, came to the same conclusion about human wisdom.

Michael Sandel recommends a different kind of humility – a recognition of our indebtedness to others, discussed in Chapter 3. Humility in this sense is an awareness, accompanied by a feeling of gratitude, that our success in life is made possible by the support of others, not only our families, teachers, and mentors, but others in our community and our larger society – people who build and maintain our homes and schools, who keep us safe, and who sustain our health. This form of humility reminds us that we are part of an extended community; we are not self-sufficient or self-made, but dependent on others for our prosperity and survival.

Humility is important in all these meanings. See also, Bruni, F. (2024). *The Age of Grievance*. Simon and Shuster.

2 Simon, P. "Still a man hears what he wants to hear and disregards the rest." *The Boxer*.

3 Nietzsche, F. (1887/2013). *On the Genealogy of Morals*. Penguin Classics.

4 James, W. (1899/2000). On a Certain Blindness in Human Beings. *Pragmatism and Other Writings*. Penguin Classics.

Chapter 12: From ideology to pragmatism: A better grammar for political debates

1 Gary Gutting calls this, the "principle of relevant evidence." Gutting, G. (2015).

2 Barrett, A. C. A Conversation with Justice Amy Coney Barrett. Catholic University of America, September 25, 2023.

3 Science, of course, can be (and often has been) misused. Science is often unable to give us definitive answers, and scientists may reach premature conclusions. Historically, pseudoscience has been used in the service of racism and genocide. This is not an indictment of science; it is a perversion of science.

4 Leonhardt, D. (2023).

5 Coleman, P. (2021).

6 French, D. (2020). *Divided We Fall: America's Secession Threat and How to Restore Our Nation*. St. Martin's Griffin.

7 French, D. *What University Presidents Got Right and Wrong about Free Speech*. New York Times, December 10, 2023.

8 Kristof, N. *Mississippi Is Offering Lessons for America on Education*. New York Times, May 31, 2023.

Chapter 13: Liberalism and conservatism in modern American politics: Pragmatic liberalism and compassionate conservatism

1 Santorum, R. (2005). *It Takes a Family: Conservatism and the Common Good*. ISI Books.

2 Gerson, M. (2007). *Heroic Conservatism*. HarperCollins.

3 Kristof, N. *When George W. Bush Was a Hero*. New York Times, April 8, 2023.

4   Gerson, M. (2007), p. 22. Gerson writes,
    "This approach [compassionate conservatism] challenges a Republican orthodoxy that is often unmoved by poverty and unwelcoming to the immigrant. And it broadens beyond the narrow passions of the Religious Right, recognizing that the Scriptures put far more emphasis on serving the poor and defenseless than on judging the behavior of our neighbors."

5   Brooks, A. C. (2017). *The Conservative Heart: How to Build a Fairer, Happier, More Prosperous America*. Broadside Books.
    Brooks notes that when conservatives argue against liberal policies, "our alternatives have generally been non-existent." This fact, however, weakens Brooks' thesis that the common understanding of conservatives as lacking compassion is a difference in perception, not of substance.

6   Brooks, A. C. (2017), p. 20.

7   Brooks, A. C. (2017), p. 173.

8   Here is another example. Brooks wants America to avoid the economic problems faced by many European countries. He warns that liberal spending will lead to stagnation, high unemployment, and the "weariness" that are now serious problems for European societies. Europe, Brooks tells us, is now in a "vortex of decline." Again, these are important concerns and facts that need to be considered. But they are not *all* the facts. European economies have both strengths and problems. In Brooks account, there is only stagnation and decline. He does not consider, for example, that Europeans are now healthier, happier, and better educated than we are, and that extreme poverty is rare. Again, we have lost an opportunity for true debate, to talk about what is both right *and* wrong with European and American economies.

9   Warren, E. (2017). *This Fight Is Our Fight: The Battle to Save Working People*. William Collins.

10 Brooks, A. C. (2017), p. 20.

11 Gopnik, A. (2019), p. 85.

12 Gopnik, A. (2019), p. 103.

13 Andrew Sullivan: The 60 Minutes Interview, November 14, 2021.

14 Sullivan, A. (2006). *The Conservative Soul: Fundamentalism, Freedom, and the Future of the American Right*. Harper Perennial. p. 250.

15 Sullivan, A. (2006), p. 268.

16 Pew Research Center, March 1, 2023.

Chapter 14: Finding common ground: The future of America's children

1 Case, A., & Deaton, A. (2020). *Deaths of Despair and the Future of Capitalism.* Princeton University Press.

2 Leonhardt, D. (2023), pp. xxiv– xxv.

3 Cass, O. (2018). *The Once and Future Worker.* Encounter Books, p. 1.

  Cass notes, "In the quarter-century prior to the Great Recession, median weekly earnings for full-time workers rose only 1 percent in real terms—not 1 percent per year, 1 percent total—and that increase was confined to women and to those with college degrees. Among all men, and among all people with less than a bachelor's degree, full-time earnings declined. While in 1979, the typical man with a high school degree could support a family of four at more than twice the poverty line, by 2007, his earnings cleared the threshold by less than 50 percent. And those are the figures for people who were working," pp. 13–14.

4 Cass, O. (2018), p. 6.

5 Cass, O. (2018), p. 2.

6 Cass, O. (2018), p. 110.

7 Putnam, R. (2015). *Our Kids: The American Dream in Crisis.* Simon and Schuster, p. 2, 7, 37.

8 Putnam reports, "...middling students are *six times more likely to graduate from college* if they come from a more affluent family (51%) than if they come from a less affluent family (8%)" (italics added). "Even more shocking, high scoring poor kids (29%) are less likely to graduate from college than low scoring rich kids (30%)," pp. 189–190.

9 Kristof, N., & WuDunn, S. (2020). *Tightrope: Americans Reaching for Hope.* Knopf, p. 17.

10 Putnam, R. (2015), p. 227.

11 Putnam, R. (2015), p. 230.

12 Putnam, R. (2015), p. 248.

13 Putnam, R. (2015), p. 251.

14 Putnam, R. (2015), p. 256.

References

Allitt, P. (2009). *The Conservative Tradition*. The Teaching Company.

Barish, K. (2021). Review of Against Empathy: The Case for Rational Compassion, by Paul Bloom. *The Humanistic Psychologist*, Vol. 49, No. 4, 630–645. https://doi.org/10.1037/hum0000181

Baron-Cohen, S. (2011). *The Science of Evil: On Empathy and the Origins of Cruelty*. Basic Books.

Barrett, A. C. *A Conversation with Justice Amy Coney Barrett*. September 25, 2023, Catholic University of America.

Baumrind, D. (1989). Rearing Competent Children. In W. Damon (Ed.). *Child Development Today and Tomorrow*. Jossey-Bass.

Bloom, P. (2016). *Against Empathy: The Case for Rational Compassion*. HarperCollins.

Bork, R. H. (1996). *Slouching toward Gomorrah: Modern Liberalism and American Decline*. HarperCollins.

Boylan, J. F. *Bring Moral Imagination Back in Style*. New York Times, July 22, 2016. see Chapter 7, Note 1 for correct italics and regular type

Brooks, A. C. (2017). *The Conservative Heart: How to Build a Fairer, Happier, More Prosperous America*. Broadside Books.

Brooks, D. *The Essential Skills for Being Human*. New York Times, October 19, 2023.

Bruni, F. (2024). *The Age of Grievance*. Simon and Shuster.

Bush, G. W. *Eulogy for Police Officers Killed in Dallas, Texas*. July 12, 2016.

Carlson, T. *Tucker Carlson Tonight*. Fox News, June 8, 2020.

Case, A. and Deaton, A. (2020). *Deaths of Despair and the Future of Capitalism*. Princeton University Press.

Cass, O. (2018). *The Once and Future Worker: A Vision for the Renewal of Work in America*. Encounter Books.

Chavez, L. (2009). *An Unlikely Conservative: The Transformation of an Ex-liberal*. Basic Books.

Chua, A. (2019). *Political Tribes: Group Instinct and the Fate of Nations*. Penguin.

Cohen, G. (2022). *Belonging: The Science of Creating Connections and Bridging Divides*. Norton.

Coleman, P. (2021). *The Way Out: How to Overcome Toxic Polarization*. Columbia University Press.

Cramer, K. (2016). *The Politics of Resentment: Rural Consciousness in Wisconsin and the Rise of Scott Walker*. University of Chicago Press.

Douthat, R. *Can Liberal and Conservative Catholics Coexist?* New York Times, May 8, 2024.

Edsall, T. *No Hate Left Behind*. New York Times, March 13, 2019.

Eisenberg, N. and Mussen, P. (1989). *The Roots of Prosocial Behavior in Children*. Cambridge University Press.

Emerson, R. W. (1841/2015). The Conservative. In *Ralph Waldo Emerson – Delphi Poets Series*. Delphi Classics.

Erikson, E. (1985). Pseudospeciation in the Nuclear Age. *Political Psychology*, Vol. 6, No. 213–217. doi: 10.2307/3790901.

Feshbach, N. (1989). Empathy Training. In J. Groebel and R. Hinde (Eds.). *Aggression and War: Their Biological and Social Bases*. Cambridge University Press, 101–111.

Finkel, E. J., et al. (October 30, 2020). Political Sectarianism in America. *Science*, Vol. 370, No. 6516, 533–536.

French, D. (2020). *Divided We Fall: America's Secession Threat and How to Restore Our Nation*. St. Matrin's Griffin.

French, D. *One Reason the Trump Fever Won't Break*. New York Times, Oct. 1, 2023.

Fukuyama, F. (2018). *Identity: The Demand for Dignity and the Politics of Resentment*. Farrar, Strauss, Giroux.

Gerson, M. (2007). *Heroic Conservatism*. HarperCollins.

Gilligan, J. (2003). Shame, Guilt, and Violence. *Social Research*, Vol. 70, No. 4, 1149–1180.

Gilovich, T. and Ross, L. (2015). *The Wisest One in the Room: How You Can Benefit from Social Psychology's Most Powerful Insights*. Free Press.

Goldwater, B. (1960/2011). *The Conscience of a Conservative*. Martino Fine Books.

Gopnik, A. (2019). *A Thousand Small Sanities: The Moral Adventure of Liberalism*. Basic Books.

Gordon, M. (2009). *Roots of Empathy: Changing the World, Child by Child*. The Experiment, LLC.

Greene, R. and Ablon, J. S. (2006). *Treating Explosive Kids*. The Guilford Press.

Gutting, G. (2015). *What Philosophy Can Do*. Norton.

Haidt, J. (2012). *The Righteous Mind: Why Good People Are Divided by Politics and Religion*. Pantheon.

Hawkins, S., Yudkin, D., Juan-Torres, M. and Dixon, T. (2018). *Hidden Tribes: A Study of America's Polarized Landscape*. More in Common. www.moreincommon.com

Heitler, S. (1993). *From Conflict to Resolution: Skills and Strategies for Individual, Couple, and Family Therapy*. W.W. Norton.

Hetherington, M. and Weiler, J. (2018). *Prius or Pickup: How the Answers to Four Simple Questions Explain America's Great Divide*. Houghton Mifflin Harcourt.

Hibbing, J. R., Smith, K. B. and Alford, J. R. (2014). *Predisposed: Liberals, Conservatives, and the Biology of Political Differences*. Routledge.

Hicks, D. (2011). *Dignity: The Essential Role It Plays in Resolving Conflict*. Yale University Press.

Hochschild, A. R. (2016). *Strangers in Their Own Land: Anger and Mourning on the American Right*. The New Press.

Holloway, J. *To Unite a Divided America, Make People Work for It*. New York Times, July 2, 2021.

Hunter, J. D. (1991). *Culture Wars: The Struggle to Define America*. Basic Books.

James, W. (1899/2000). On a Certain Blindness in Human Beings. In *Pragmatism and Other Writings*. Penguin Classics.

James, W. (1907/2000). *Pragmatism and Other Writings*. Penguin Classics.

Jost, J. T., Federico, C. M. and Napier, J. L. (2009). Political Ideology: Its Structure, Functions, and Elective Affinities. *Annual Review of Psychology*, Vol. 60, 307–337.

Kagan, D. (1995). *On the Origins of War*. Doubleday.

Kahneman, D. (2023). Adversarial Collaboration. An EDGE Lecture. https://www.edge.org/adversarial-collaboration-daniel-kahneman

Kelman, H. (2017). *Resolving Deep-Rooted Conflicts: Essays on the Theory and Practice of Interactive Problem-Solving* (Ed. W. Wintersteiner and W. Graf). Routledge.

Kessler, D. (2017). *Capture: Unraveling the Mystery of Mental Suffering.* HarperCollins.

Kristof, N. and WuDunn, S. (2020). *Tightrope: Americans Reaching for Hope.* Knopf.

Krugman, P. *Good Economy, Negative Vibes: The Story Continues.* New York Times, April 8, 2024.

Lakoff, G. (2002). *Moral Politics,* 2nd ed. University of Chicago Press.

Lakoff, G. (2009). *The Political Mind.* Penguin.

Leonhardt, D. (2023). *Ours Was the Shining Future: The Story of the American Dream.* Random House.

Levin, Y. (2014). *The Great Debate: Edmund Burke, Thomas Paine, and the Birth of Right and Left.* Basic Books.

Locke, J. (1689/1996). *An Essay Concerning Human Understanding.* Hackett Publishing.

Lukianoff, G. and Haidt, J. (2018). *The Coddling of the American Mind: How Good Intentions and Bad Ideas Are Setting Up a Generation for Failure.* Penguin Books.

Mascolo, M. F. (2024). Toward a More Collaborative Democracy: Bridging Political Divides through Dialectical Problem-Solving. In N. Shannon, M. F. Mascolo, and A. Belolutskaya (Eds.). *Routledge International Handbook of Dialectical Thinking.* Routledge, 353–373.

McCarten, A. (2019). *The Two Popes: Francis, Benedict, and the Decision that Shook the World.* Flatiron Books.

Murthy, V. H. (2020) *Together: Loneliness, Health, and What Happens When We Find Connection.* HarperCollins.

Nguyen, J. *Governor Cox Gives Emotional Stance on Bill Targeting Transgender Youth.* ABC4.com, February 18, 2021.

Nietzsche, F. (1887/2013). *On the Genealogy of Morals.* Penguin Classics.

Nilsson, A. and Jost, J. T. (2020). Rediscovering Tomkins' Polarity Theory: Humanism, Normativism, and the Psychological Basis of Left-Right Ideological Conflict in the U.S. and Sweden. *PLOS ONE,* Vol.15, No.7, e0236627.

Nocera, J. *The Ugliness Started with Bork.* New York Times, October 21, 2011.

Nussbaum, M. (2018). *The Monarchy of Fear: A Philosopher Looks at Our Political Crisis.* Simon and Schuster.

Nussbaum, M. (2004). *Hiding from Humanity: Disgust, Shame, and the Law.* Princeton University Press.

Obama, B. *Eulogy for Police Officers Killed in Dallas. Texas,* July 12, 2016.

Pink, D. H. (2018). *When: The Scientific Secrets of Perfect Timing*. Riverhead Books.

Putnam, R. (2001). *Bowling Alone: The Collapse and Revival of American Community*. Simon and Shuster.

Putnam, R. (2015). *Our Kids: The American Dream in Crisis*. Simon and Schuster.

Putnam, R. (2020). *The Upswing: How America Came Together a Century Ago and How We Can Do It Again*. Simon and Schuster.

Pyszczynski, T., Solomon, S. and Greenberg, J. (2015). Thirty Years of Terror Management Theory: From Genesis to Revelation. *Advances in Experimental Social Psychology*, Vol. 52, 1–70. ISSN 0065-2601 http://dx.doi.org/10.1016/bs.aesp.2015.03.001

Ramiah, A. A. and Hewstone, M. (2013). Intergroup Contact as a Tool for Reducing, Resolving, and Preventing Intergroup Conflict. *American Psychologist*, Vol. 68, No. 7, 527–542. DOI: 10.1037/a0032603

Reich, R. B. (2018). *The Common Good*. Knopf.

Robin, C. (2018). *The Reactionary Mind: Conservatism from Edmund Burke to Donald Trump*. Oxford University Press.

Sandel, M. J. (2020). *The Tyranny of Merit: What's Become of the Common Good*. Farrar, Strauss and Giroux.

Santorum, R. (2005). *It Takes a Family: Conservatism and the Common Good*. ISI Books.

Scheff, T. J. and Ratzinger, S. M. (1991). *Emotions and Violence: Shame and Rage in Destructive Conflicts*. Authors Guild Backinprint.com.

Smith, A. (1790/2009). *The Theory of Moral Sentiments*. Penguin.

Smith, S. B. (2021). *Reclaiming Patriotism in an Age of Extremes*. Yale University Press.

Solomon, A. *My Book Was Censored in China. Now It's Blacklisted – in Texas*. New York Times, November 23, 2021.

Sowell, T. (2007). *A Conflict of Visions: Ideological Origins of Political Struggles, Revised* ed. Basic Books.

Stenner, K. (2005). *The Authoritarian Dynamic*. Cambridge University Press.

Sullivan, A. (2006). *The Conservative Soul: Fundamentalism, Freedom, and the Future of the American Right*. Harper Perennial.

Sullivan, A. *Andrew Sullivan: The 60 Minutes Interview*. November 14, 2021. CBS

Sulloway, F. J. (1996). *Born to Rebel: Birth Order, Family Dynamics, and Creative Lives*. Vintage Books.

Tangney, J. P., and Fischer, K. W. (Eds.) (1995). *Self-Conscious Emotions: The Psychology of Shame, Guilt, Embarrassment, and Pride.* The Guilford Press.

Time Magazine, *Essay: The Homosexual in America.* January 21, 1966.

Tomkins, S. S. (1995). *Exploring Affect: The Selected Writings of Sylvan S. Tomkins* (Ed. E. Virginia Demos). Cambridge University Press.

Tuschman, A. (2013). *Our Political Nature: The Evolutionary Origins of What Divides Us.* Prometheus Books.

University of Michigan. (2021). *Study: Evolution Now Accepted by Majority of Americans.* Michigan News, August, 20, 2021.

Volkan, V. (1994). *The Need to Have Enemies and Allies: From Clinical Practice to International Relationships.* Jason Aronson.

Volkan, V. (1997). *Blood Lines: From Ethnic Pride to Ethnic Cleansing.* Westview Press.

Warren, E. (2017). *This Fight Is Our Fight: The Battle to Save Working People.* William Collins.

Will, G. (2019). *The Conservative Sensibility.* Hachette Books.

Yancy, G. (2022). *Beyond Racial Division: A Unifying Alternative to Colorblindness and Antiracism.* Intervarsity Press.

Yankelovich, D. (1999). *The Magic of Dialogue: Transforming Conflict into Cooperation.* Simon and Schuster.

Zaki, J. (2020). *The War for Kindness: Building Empathy in a Fractured World.* Broadway Books.

Index